United States Laws

Import Duties of the United States

The Tariff Act approved July 24, 1897

United States Laws

Import Duties of the United States
The Tariff Act approved July 24, 1897

ISBN/EAN: 9783337232856

Printed in Europe, USA, Canada, Australia, Japan

Cover: Foto ©Suzi / pixelio.de

More available books at **www.hansebooks.com**

IMPORT DUTIES OF THE UNITED STATES.

THE TARIFF ACT APPROVED JULY 24, 1897.

FIFTY-FIFTH CONGRESS, FIRST SESSION.

BUREAU OF AMERICAN REPUBLICS,
INTERNATIONAL UNION OF AMERICAN REPUBLICS,
WASHINGTON, U. S. A.

JOSEPH P. SMITH, Director.

Bulletin No. 75,
JULY, 1897.

WASHINGTON:
GOVERNMENT PRINTING OFFICE.
1897.

An Act To provide revenue for the Government and to encourage the industries of the United States.

Be it enacted by the Senate and House of Representatives of the United States of America in Congress assembled, That on and after the passage of this Act, unless otherwise specially provided for in this Act, there shall be levied, collected, and paid upon all articles imported from foreign countries, and mentioned in the schedules herein contained, the rates of duty which are, by the schedules and paragraphs, respectively prescribed, namely:

SCHEDULE A.—CHEMICALS, OILS, AND PAINTS.

1. ACIDS: Acetic or pyroligneous acid, not exceeding the specific gravity of one and forty-seven one-thousandths, three-fourths of one cent per pound; exceeding the specific gravity of one and forty-seven one-thousandths, two cents per pound; boracic acid, five cents per pound; chromic acid and lactic acid, three cents per pound; citric acid, seven cents per pound; salicylic acid, ten cents per pound; sulphuric acid or oil of vitriol not specially provided for in this Act, one-fourth of one cent per pound; tannic acid or tannin, fifty cents per pound; gallic acid, ten cents per pound; tartaric acid, seven cents per pound; all other acids not specially provided for in this Act, twenty-five per centum ad valorem.

2. All alcoholic perfumery, including cologne water and other toilet waters and toilet preparations of all kinds, containing alcohol or in the preparation of which alcohol is used, and alcoholic compounds not specially provided for in this Act, sixty cents per pound and forty-five per centum ad valorem.

3. Alkalies, alkaloids, distilled oils, essential oils, expressed oils, rendered oils, and all combinations of the foregoing, and all chemical compounds and salts not specially provided for in this Act, twenty-five per centum ad valorem.

4. Alumina, hydrate of, or refined bauxite, six-tenths of one cent per pound; alum, alum cake, patent alum, sulphate of alumina, and aluminous cake, and alum in crystals or ground, one-half of one cent per pound.

5. Ammonia, carbonate of, one and one-half cents per pound; muriate of, or sal ammoniac, three-fourths of one cent per pound; sulphate of, three-tenths of one cent per pound.

6. Argols or crude tartar or wine lees crude, containing not more than forty per centum of bitartrate of potash, one cent per pound; containing more than forty per centum of bitartrate of potash, one and one-half cents per pound; tartars and lees crystals, or partly refined argols, containing not more than ninety per centum of bitartrate of potash, and tartrate of soda or potassa, or Rochelle salts, four cents per pound; containing more than ninety per centum of bitartrate of potash, five cents per pound; cream of tartar and patent tartar, six cents per pound.

7. Blacking of all kinds, twenty-five per centum ad valorem.

8. Bleaching powder, or chloride of lime, one-fifth of one cent per pound.

9. Blue vitriol or sulphate of copper, one-half of one cent per pound.

10. Bone char, suitable for use in decolorizing sugars, twenty per centum ad valorem.

11. Borax, five cents per pound; borates of lime or soda, or other borate material not otherwise provided for, containing more than thirty-six per centum of anhydrous boracic acid, four cents per pound; borates of lime or soda, or other borate material not otherwise provided for, containing not more than thirty-six per centum of anhydrous boracic acid, three cents per pound.

12. Camphor, refined, six cents per pound.

13. Chalk (not medicinal nor prepared for toilet purposes) when ground, precipitated naturally or artificially, or otherwise prepared, whether in the form of cubes, blocks, sticks or disks, or otherwise, including tailors', billiard, red, or French chalk, one cent per pound. Manufactures of chalk not specially provided for in this Act, twenty-five per centum ad valorem.

14. Chloroform, twenty cents per pound.

15. Coal-tar dyes or colors, not specially provided for in this Act, thirty per centum ad valorem; all other products or preparations of coal tar, not colors or dyes and not medicinal, not specially provided for in this Act, twenty per centum ad valorem.

16. Cobalt, oxide of, twenty-five cents per pound.

17. Collodion and all compounds of pyroxylin, whether known as celluloid or by any other name, fifty cents per pound; rolled or in sheets, unpolished, and not made up into articles, sixty cents per pound; if in finished or partly finished articles, and articles of which collodion or any compound of pyroxylin is the component material of chief value, sixty-five cents per pound and twenty-five per centum ad valorem.

18. Coloring for brandy, wine, beer, or other liquors, fifty per centum ad valorem.

19. Copperas or sulphate of iron, one-fourth of one cent per pound.

20. Drugs, such as barks, beans, berries, balsams, buds, bulbs, bulbous roots, excrescences, fruits, flowers, dried fibers, dried insects, grains, gums and gum resin, herbs, leaves, lichens, mosses, nuts, nutgalls, roots, stems, spices, vegetables, seeds (aromatic, not garden seeds), seeds of morbid growth, weeds, and woods used expressly for dyeing; any of the foregoing which are drugs and not edible, but which are advanced in value or condition by refining, grinding, or other process, and not specially provided for in this Act, one-fourth of one cent per pound, and in addition thereto ten per centum ad valorem.

21. Ethers: Sulphuric, forty cents per pound; spirits of nitrous ether, twenty-five cents per pound; fruit ethers, oils, or essences, two dollars per pound; ethers of all kinds not specially provided for in this Act, one dollar per pound: *Provided*, That no article of this paragraph shall pay a less rate of duty than twenty-five per centum ad valorem.

22. Extracts and decoctions of logwood and other dyewoods, and extracts of barks, such as are commonly used for dyeing or tanning, not specially provided for in this Act, seven-eighths of one cent per pound; extracts of quebracho and of hemlock bark, one-half of one cent per pound; extracts of sumac, and of woods other than dyewoods, not specially provided for in this Act, five-eighths of one cent per pound.

23. Gelatin, glue, isinglass or fish glue, and prepared fish bladders or fish sounds, valued at not above ten cents per pound, two and one-

half cents per pound; valued at above ten cents per pound and not above thirty-five cents per pound, twenty-five per centum ad valorem; valued above thirty-five cents per pound, fifteen cents per pound and twenty per centum ad valorem.

24. Glycerin, crude, not purified, one cent per pound; refined, three cents per pound.

25. Indigo, extracts, or pastes of, three-fourths of one cent per pound; carmined, ten cents per pound.

26. Ink and ink powders, twenty-five per centum ad valorem.

27. Iodine, resublimed, twenty cents per pound.

28. Iodoform, one dollar per pound.

29. Licorice, extracts of, in paste, rolls, or other forms, four and one-half cents per pound.

30. Chicle, ten cents per pound.

31. Magnesia, carbonate of, medicinal, three cents per pound; calcined, medicinal, seven cents per pound; sulphate of, or Epsom salts, one-fifth of one cent per pound.

OILS:

32. Alizarin assistant, sulpho-ricinoleic acid, and ricinoleic acid, by whatever name known, whether liquid, solid, or in paste, in the manufacture of which fifty per centum or more of castor oil is used, thirty cents per gallon; in the manufacture of which less than fifty per centum of castor oil is used, fifteen cents per gallon; all other alizarin assistant, not specially provided for in this Act, thirty per centum ad valorem.

33. Castor oil, thirty-five cents per gallon.

34. Cod-liver oil, fifteen cents per gallon.

35. Cotton-seed oil, four cents per gallon of seven and one-half pounds weight.

36. Croton oil, twenty cents per pound.

37. Flaxseed, linseed, and poppy-seed oil, raw, boiled, or oxidized, twenty cents per gallon of seven and one-half pounds weight.

38. Fusel oil, or amylic alcohol, one-fourth of one cent per pound.

39. Hemp-seed oil and rape-seed oil, ten cents per gallon.

40. Olive oil, not specially provided for in this Act, forty cents per gallon; in bottles, jars, tins, or similar packages, fifty cents per gallon.

41. Peppermint oil, fifty cents per pound.

42. Seal, herring, whale, and other fish oil, not specially provided for in this Act, eight cents per gallon.

43. Opium, crude or unmanufactured, and not adulterated, containing nine per centum and over of morphia, one dollar per pound; morphia or morphine, sulphate of, and all alkaloids or salts of opium, one dollar per ounce; aqueous extract of opium, for medicinal uses, and tincture of, as laudanum, and other liquid preparations of opium, not specially provided for in this Act, forty per centum ad valorem; opium containing less than nine per centum of morphia, and opium prepared for smoking, six dollars per pound; but opium prepared for smoking and other preparations of opium deposited in bonded warehouses shall not be removed therefrom without payment of duties, and such duties shall not be refunded.

PAINTS, COLORS, AND VARNISHES:

44. Baryta, sulphate of, or barytes, including barytes earth, unmanufactured, seventy-five cents per ton; manufactured, five dollars and twenty-five cents per ton.

45. Blues, such as Berlin, Prussian, Chinese, and all others, containing ferrocyanide of iron, in pulp, dry or ground in or mixed with oil or water, eight cents per pound.
46. Blanc-fixe, or artificial sulphate of barytes, and satin white, or artificial sulphate of lime, one-half of one cent per pound.
47. Black, made from bone, ivory, or vegetable substance, by whatever name known, including bone black and lampblack, dry or ground in oil or water, twenty-five per centum ad valorem.
48. Chrome yellow, chrome green, and all other chromium colors in the manufacture of which lead and bichromate of potash or soda are used, in pulp, dry, or ground in or mixed with oil or water, four and one-half cents per pound.
49. Ocher and ochery earths, sienna and sienna earths, and umber and umber earths, not specially provided for, when crude or not powdered, washed or pulverized, one-eighth of one cent per pound; if powdered, washed or pulverized, three-eighths of one cent per pound; if ground in oil or water, one and one-half cents per pound.
50. Orange mineral, three and three-eighths cents per pound.
51. Red lead, two and seven-eighths cents per pound.
52. Ultramarine blue, whether dry, in pulp, or mixed with water, and wash blue containing ultramarine, three and three-fourths cents per pound.
53. Varnishes, including so-called gold size or japan, thirty-five per centum ad valorem; spirit varnishes, one dollar and thirty-two cents per gallon and thirty-five per centum ad valorem.
54. Vermilion red, and other colors containing quicksilver, dry or ground in oil or water, ten cents per pound; when not containing quicksilver but made of lead or containing lead, five cents per pound.
55. White lead, white paint and pigment containing lead, dry or in pulp, or ground or mixed with oil, two and seven-eighths cents per pound.
56. Whiting and Paris white, dry, one-fourth of one cent per pound; ground in oil, or putty, one cent per pound.
57. Zinc, oxide of, and white paint or pigment containing zinc, but not containing lead, dry, one cent per pound; ground in oil, one and three-fourth cents per pound; sulfid of zinc white, or white sulphide of zinc, one and one-fourth cents per pound; chloride of zinc and sulphate of zinc, one cent per pound.
58. All paints, colors, pigments, lakes, crayons, smalts and frostings, whether crude or dry or mixed, or ground with water or oil or with solutions other than oil, not otherwise specially provided for in this Act, thirty per centum ad valorem; all paints, colors and pigments, commonly known as artists' paints or colors, whether in tubes, pans, cakes or other forms, thirty per centum ad valorem.
59. Paris green, and London purple, fifteen per centum ad valorem.
60. Lead: Acetate of, white, three and one-fourth cents per pound; brown, gray, or yellow, two and one-fourth cents per pound; nitrate of, two and one-half cents per pound; litharge, two and three-fourth cents per pound.
61. Phosphorus, eighteen cents per pound.

POTASH:
62. Bichromate and chromate of, three cents per pound.
63. Caustic or hydrate of, refined, in sticks or rolls, one cent per pound; chlorate of, two and one-half cents per pound.

64. Hydriodate, iodide, and iodate of, twenty-five cents per pound.
65. Nitrate of, or saltpeter, refined, one-half cent per pound.
66. Prussiate of, red, eight cents per pound; yellow, four cents per pound; cyanide of potassium, twelve and one-half per centum ad valorem.

PREPARATIONS:
67. Medicinal preparations containing alcohol, or in the preparation of which alcohol is used, not specially provided for in this Act, fifty-five cents per pound, but in no case shall the same pay less than twenty-five per centum ad valorem.
68. Medicinal preparations not containing alcohol or in the preparation of which alcohol is not used, not specially provided for in this Act, twenty-five per centum ad valorem; calomel and other mercurial medicinal preparations, thirty-five per centum ad valorem.
69. Plasters, healing or curative, of all kinds, and court-plaster, thirty-five per centum ad valorem.
70. Preparations used as applications to the hair, mouth, teeth, or skin, such as cosmetics, dentifrices, pastes, pomades, powders, and other toilet articles, and articles of perfumery, whether in sachets or otherwise, not containing alcohol or in the manufacture of which alcohol is not used, and not specially provided for in this Act, fifty per centum ad valorem.
71. Santonin, and all salts thereof containing eighty per centum or over of santonin, one dollar per pound.

SOAP:
72. Castile soap, one and one-fourth cents per pound; fancy, perfumed, and all descriptions of toilet soap, including so-called medicinal or medicated soaps, fifteen cents per pound; all other soaps not specially provided for in this Act, twenty per centum ad valorem.

SODA:
73. Bicarbonate of soda, or supercarbonate of soda, or saleratus, and other alkalies containing fifty per centum or more of bicarbonate of soda, three-fourths of one cent per pound.
74. Bichromate and chromate of soda, two cents per pound.
75. Crystal carbonate of soda, or concentrated soda crystals, or monohydrate, or sesquicarbonate of soda, three-tenths of one cent per pound; chlorate of soda two cents per pound.
76. Hydrate of, or caustic soda, three-fourths of one cent per pound; nitrite of soda, two and one-half cents per pound; hypo-sulphite and sulphide of soda, one-half of one cent per pound.
77. Sal soda, or soda crystals, not concentrated, two-tenths of one cent per pound.
78. Soda ash, three-eighths of one cent per pound; arseniate of soda, one and one-fourth cents per pound.
79. Silicate of soda, or other alkaline silicate, one-half of one cent per pound.
80. Sulphate of soda, or salt cake, or niter cake, one dollar and twenty-five cents per ton.
81. Sea moss, ten per centum ad valorem.
82. Sponges, twenty per centum ad valorem; manufactures of sponges, or of which sponge is the component material of chief value, not specially provided for in this Act, forty per centum ad valorem.

83. Strychnia, or strychnine, and all salts thereof, thirty cents per ounce.
84. Sulphur, refined or sublimed, or flowers of, eight dollars per ton.
85. Sumac, ground, three-tenths of one cent per pound.
86. Vanillin, eighty cents per ounce.

SCHEDULE B.—EARTHS, EARTHENWARE, AND GLASSWARE.

BRICK AND TILE:
87. Fire-brick, weighing not more than ten pounds each, not glazed, enameled, ornamented, or decorated in any manner, one dollar and twenty-five cents per ton; glazed, enameled, ornamented, or decorated, forty-five per centum ad valorem; brick, other than fire-brick, not glazed, enameled, painted, vitrified, ornamented, or decorated in any manner, twenty-five per centum ad valorem; if glazed, enameled, painted, vitrified, ornamented, or decorated in any manner, forty-five per centum ad valorem.
88. Tiles, plain unglazed, one color, exceeding two square inches in size, four cents per square foot; glazed, encaustic, ceramic mosaic, vitrified, semi-vitrified, flint, spar, embossed, enameled, ornamental, hand painted, gold decorated, and all other earthenware tiles, valued at not exceeding forty cents per square foot, eight cents per square foot; exceeding forty cents per square foot, ten cents per square foot and twenty-five per centum ad valorem.

CEMENT, LIME, AND PLASTER:
89. Roman, Portland, and other hydraulic cement, in barrels, sacks, or other packages, eight cents per one hundred pounds, including weight of barrel or package; in bulk, seven cents per one hundred pounds; other cement, twenty per centum ad valorem.
90. Lime, five cents per one hundred pounds, including weight of barrel or package.
91. Plaster rock or gypsum, crude, fifty cents per ton; if ground or calcined, two dollars and twenty-five cents per ton; pearl hardening for paper makers' use, twenty per centum ad valorem.
92. Pumice stone, wholly or partially manufactured, six dollars per ton; unmanufactured, fifteen per centum ad valorem.

CLAYS OR EARTHS:
93. Clays or earths, unwrought or unmanufactured, not specially provided for in this Act, one dollar per ton; wrought or manufactured, not specially provided for in this Act, two dollars per ton; china clay or kaolin, two dollars and fifty cents per ton; limestone rock asphalt containing not more than fifteen per centum of bitumen, fifty cents per ton; asphaltum and bitumen, not specially provided for in this Act, crude, if not dried, or otherwise advanced in any manner, one dollar and fifty cents per ton; if dried or otherwise advanced in any manner, three dollars per ton; bauxite, or beauxite, crude, not refined or otherwise advanced in condition from its natural state, one dollar per ton; fullers' earth, unwrought and unmanufactured, one dollar and fifty cents per ton; wrought or manufactured, three dollars per ton.

EARTHENWARE AND CHINA:
94. Common yellow, brown, or gray earthenware, plain, embossed, or salt-glazed common stoneware, and crucibles, all the foregoing not decorated in any manner, twenty-five per centum ad valorem; Rockingham earthenware not decorated, forty per centum ad valorem.
95. China, porcelain, parian, bisque, earthen, stone, and crockery ware, including clock cases with or without movements, plaques, ornaments, toys, toy tea sets, charms, vases and statuettes, painted, tinted, stained, enameled, printed, gilded, or otherwise decorated or ornamented in any manner, sixty per centum ad valorem; if plain white and without superadded ornamentation of any kind, fifty-five per centum ad valorem.
96. All other china, porcelain, parian, bisque, earthen, stone, and crockery ware, and manufactures thereof, or of which the same is the component material of chief value, by whatever name known, not specially provided for in this Act, if painted, tinted, stained, enameled, printed, gilded, or otherwise decorated or ornamented in any manner, sixty per centum ad valorem; if not ornamented or decorated, fifty-five per centum ad valorem.
97. Articles and wares composed wholly or in chief value of earthy or mineral substances, or carbon, not specially provided for in this Act, if not decorated in any manner, thirty-five per centum ad valorem; if decorated, forty-five per centum ad valorem.
98. Gas retorts, three dollars each; lava tips for burners, ten cents per gross and fifteen per centum ad valorem; carbons for electric lighting, ninety cents per hundred; filter tubes, forty-five per centum ad valorem; porous carbon pots for electric batteries, without metallic connections, twenty per centum ad valorem.

GLASS AND GLASSWARE:
99. Plain green or colored, molded or pressed, and flint, lime, or lead glass bottles, vials, jars, and covered or uncovered demijohns and carboys, any of the foregoing, filled or unfilled, not otherwise specially provided for, and whether their contents be dutiable or free, (except such as contain merchandise subject to an ad valorem rate of duty, or to a rate of duty based in whole or in part upon the value thereof, which shall be dutiable at the rate applicable to their contents) shall pay duty as follows: If holding more than one pint, one cent per pound; if holding not more than one pint and not less than one-fourth of a pint, one and one-half cents per pound; if holding less than one-fourth of a pint, fifty cents per gross: Provided, That none of the above articles shall pay a less rate of duty than forty per centum ad valorem.
100. Glass bottles, decanters, or other vessels or articles of glass, cut, engraved, painted, colored, stained, silvered, gilded, etched, frosted, printed in any manner or otherwise ornamented, decorated, or ground (except such grinding as is necessary for fitting stoppers), and any articles of which such glass is the component material of chief value, and porcelain, opal and other blown glassware; all the foregoing, filled or unfilled, and whether their contents be dutiable or free, sixty per centum ad valorem.

101. Unpolished, cylinder, crown, and common window glass, not exceeding ten by fifteen inches square, one and three-eighths cents per pound; above that, and not exceeding sixteen by twenty-four inches square, one and seven-eighths cents per pound; above that, and not exceeding twenty-four by thirty inches square, two and three-eighths cents per pound; above that, and not exceeding twenty-four by thirty-six inches square, two and seven-eighths cents per pound; above that, and not exceeding thirty by forty inches square, three and three-eighths cents per pound; above that, and not exceeding forty by sixty inches square, three and seven-eighths cents per pound; above that, four and three-eighths cents per pound: *Provided*, That unpolished cylinder, crown, and common window glass, imported in boxes, shall contain fifty square feet, as nearly as sizes will permit, and the duty shall be computed thereon according to the actual weight of glass.

102. Cylinder and crown glass, polished, not exceeding sixteen by twenty-four inches square, four cents per square foot; above that, and not exceeding twenty-four by thirty inches square, six cents per square foot; above that, and not exceeding twenty-four by sixty inches square, fifteen cents per square foot; above that, twenty cents per square foot.

103. Fluted, rolled, ribbed, or rough plate glass, or the same containing a wire netting within itself, not including crown, cylinder, or common window glass, not exceeding sixteen by twenty-four inches square, three-fourths of one cent per square foot; above that, and not exceeding twenty-four by thirty inches square, one and one-fourth cents per square foot; all above that, one and three-fourths cents per square foot; and all fluted, rolled, ribbed, or rough plate glass, weighing over one hundred pounds per one hundred square feet, shall pay an additional duty on the excess at the same rates herein imposed: *Provided*, That all of the above plate glass, when ground, smoothed, or otherwise obscured, shall be subject to the same rate of duty as cast polished plate glass unsilvered.

104. Cast polished plate glass, finished or unfinished and unsilvered, not exceeding sixteen by twenty-four inches square, eight cents per square foot; above that, and not exceeding twenty-four by thirty inches square, ten cents per square foot; above that, and not exceeding twenty-four by sixty inches square, twenty-two and one-half cents per square foot; all above that, thirty-five cents per square foot.

105. Cast polished plate glass, silvered, cylinder and crown glass, silvered, and looking-glass plates, exceeding in size one hundred and forty-four square inches and not exceeding sixteen by twenty-four inches square, eleven cents per square foot; above that, and not exceeding twenty-four by thirty inches square, thirteen cents per square foot; above that, and not exceeding twenty-four by sixty inches square, twenty-five cents per square foot; all above that, thirty-eight cents per square foot.

106. But no looking-glass plates or plate glass, silvered, when framed, shall pay a less rate of duty than that imposed upon similar glass of like description not framed, but shall pay in addition thereto upon such frames the rate of duty applicable thereto when imported separate.

107. Cast polished plate glass, silvered or unsilvered, and cylinder, crown, or common window glass, silvered or unsilvered, when bent, ground, obscured, frosted, sanded, enameled, beveled, etched, embossed, engraved, flashed, stained, colored, painted, or otherwise ornamented or decorated, shall be subject to a duty of five per centum ad valorem in addition to the rates otherwise chargeable thereon.

108. Spectacles, eyeglasses, and goggles, and frames for the same, or parts thereof, finished or unfinished, valued at not over forty cents per dozen, twenty cents per dozen and fifteen per centum ad valorem; valued at over forty cents per dozen and not over one dollar and fifty cents per dozen, forty-five cents per dozen and twenty per centum ad valorem; valued at over one dollar and fifty cents per dozen, fifty per centum ad valorem.

109. Lenses of glass or pebble, ground and polished to a spherical, cylindrical, or prismatic form, and ground and polished plano or coquill glasses, wholly or partly manufactured, with the edges unground, forty-five per centum ad valorem; if with their edges ground or beveled, ten cents per dozen pairs and forty-five per centum ad valorem.

110. Strips of glass, not more than three inches wide, ground or polished on one or both sides to a cylindrical or prismatic form, and glass slides for magic lanterns, forty-five per centum ad valorem.

111. Opera and field glasses, telescopes, microscopes, photographic and projecting lenses and optical instruments, and frames or mountings for the same; all the foregoing not specially provided for in this Act, forty-five per centum ad valorem.

112. Stained or painted glass windows, or parts thereof, and all mirrors, not exceeding in size one hundred and forty-four square inches, with or without frames or cases, and all glass or manufactures of glass or paste, or of which glass or paste is the component material of chief value, not specially provided for in this Act, forty-five per centum ad valorem.

113. Fusible enamel, twenty-five per centum ad valorem.

MARBLE AND STONE, AND MANUFACTURES OF:

114. Marble in block, rough or squared only, sixty-five cents per cubic foot; onyx in block, rough or squared, one dollar and fifty cents per cubic foot; marble or onyx, sawed or dressed, over two inches in thickness, one dollar and ten cents per cubic foot; slabs or paving tiles of marble or onyx, containing not less than four superficial inches, if not more than one inch in thickness, twelve cents per superficial foot; if more than one inch and not more than one and one-half inches in thickness, fifteen cents per superficial foot; if more than one and one-half inches and not more than two inches in thickness, eighteen cents per superficial foot; if rubbed in whole or in part, three cents per superficial foot in addition; mosaic cubes of marble, onyx, or stone, not exceeding two cubic inches in size, if loose, one cent per pound and twenty per centum ad valorem; if attached to paper or other material, twenty cents per superficial foot and thirty-five per centum ad valorem.

115. Manufactures of agate, alabaster, chalcedony, chrysolite, coral, cornelian, garnet, jasper, jet, malachite, marble, onyx, rock crystal, or spar, including clock cases with or without

movements, not specially provided for in this Act, fifty per centum ad valorem.

Stone—

116. Burr stones, manufactured or bound up into millstones, fifteen per centum ad valorem.

117. Freestone, granite, sandstone, limestone, and other building or monumental stone, except marble and onyx, unmanufactured or undressed, not specially provided for in this Act, twelve cents per cubic foot.

118. Freestone, granite, sandstone, limestone, and other building or monumental stone, except marble and onyx, not specially provided for in this Act, hewn, dressed, or polished, fifty per centum ad valorem.

119. Grindstones, finished or unfinished, one dollar and seventy-five cents per ton.

Slate—

120. Slates, slate chimney-pieces, mantels, slabs for tables, roofing slates, and all other manufactures of slate, not specially provided for in this Act, twenty per centum ad valorem.

SCHEDULE C.—METALS AND MANUFACTURES OF.

121. Iron ore, including manganiferous iron ore, and the dross or residuum from burnt pyrites, forty cents per ton: *Provided*, That in levying and collecting the duty on iron ore no deduction shall be made from the weight of the ore on account of moisture which may be chemically or physically combined therewith; basic slag, ground or unground, one dollar per ton.

122. Iron in pigs, iron kentledge, spiegeleisen, ferro-manganese, ferrosilicon, wrought and cast scrap iron, and scrap steel, four dollars per ton; but nothing shall be deemed scrap iron or scrap steel except waste or refuse iron or steel fit only to be remanufactured.

123. Bar iron, square iron, rolled or hammered, comprising flats not less than one inch wide nor less than three-eighths of one inch thick, round iron not less than seven-sixteenths of one inch in diameter, sixtenths of one cent per pound.

124. Round iron, in coils or rods, less than seven-sixteenths of one inch in diameter, and bars or shapes of rolled or hammered iron, not specially provided for in this Act, eight-tenths of one cent per pound: *Provided*, That all iron in slabs, blooms, loops, or other forms less finished than iron in bars, and more advanced than pig iron, except castings, shall be subject to a duty of five-tenths of one cent per pound: *Provided further*, That all iron bars, blooms, billets, or sizes or shapes of any kind, in the manufacture of which charcoal is used as fuel, shall be subject to a duty of twelve dollars per ton.

125. Beams, girders, joists, angles, channels, car-truck channels, T T, columns and posts or parts or sections of columns and posts, deck and bulb beams, and building forms, together with all other structural shapes of iron or steel, whether plain or punched, or fitted for use, five-tenths of one cent per pound.

126. Boiler or other plate iron or steel, except crucible plate steel and saw plates hereinafter provided for, not thinner than number ten wire gauge, sheared or unsheared, and skelp iron or steel sheared or rolled in grooves, valued at one cent per pound or less, five-tenths of one cent per pound; valued above one cent and not above two cents per pound, six-tenths of one cent per pound; valued above two cents and not above

four cents per pound, one cent per pound; valued at over four cents per pound, twenty-five per centum ad valorem: *Provided*, That all sheets or plates of iron or steel thinner than number ten wire gauge shall pay duty as iron or steel sheets.

127. Iron or steel anchors or parts thereof, one and one-half cents per pound; forgings of iron or steel, or of combined iron and steel, of whatever shape or whatever degree or stage of manufacture, not specially provided for in this Act, thirty-five per centum ad valorem; antifriction ball forgings of iron or steel, or of combined iron and steel, forty-five per centum ad valorem.

128. Hoop, band, or scroll iron or steel, not otherwise provided for in this Act, valued at three cents per pound or less, eight inches or less in width, and less than three-eighths of one inch thick and not thinner than number ten wire gauge, five-tenths of one cent per pound; thinner than number ten wire gauge and not thinner than number twenty wire gauge, six-tenths of one cent per pound; thinner than number twenty wire gauge, eight-tenths of one cent per pound: *Provided*, That barrel hoops of iron or steel, and hoop or band iron or hoop or band steel flared, splayed or punched, with or without buckles or fastenings, shall pay one-tenth of one cent per pound more duty than that imposed on the hoop or band iron or steel from which they are made; steel bands or strips, untempered, suitable for making band saws, three cents per pound and twenty per centum ad valorem; if tempered, or tempered and polished, six cents per pound and twenty per centum ad valorem.

129. Hoop or band iron, or hoop or band steel, cut to lengths, or wholly or partly manufactured into hoops or ties, coated or not coated with paint or any other preparation, with or without buckles or fastenings, for baling cotton or any other commodity, five-tenths of one cent per pound.

130. Railway bars, made of iron or steel, and railway bars made in part of steel, T rails, and punched iron or steel flat rails, seven-twentieths of one cent per pound; railway fish-plates or splice-bars, made of iron or steel, four-tenths of one cent per pound.

131. Sheets of iron or steel, common or black, of whatever dimensions, and skelp iron or steel, valued at three cents per pound or less, thinner than number ten and not thinner than number twenty wire gauge, seven-tenths of one cent per pound; thinner than number twenty wire gauge and not thinner than number twenty-five wire gauge, eight-tenths of one cent per pound; thinner than number twenty-five wire gauge and not thinner than number thirty-two wire gauge, one and one-tenth cents per pound; thinner than number thirty-two wire gauge, one and two-tenths cents per pound; corrugated or crimped, one and one-tenth cents per pound: *Provided*, That all sheets of common or black iron or steel not thinner than number ten wire gauge shall pay duty as plate iron or plate steel.

132. All iron or steel sheets or plates, and all hoop, band, or scroll iron or steel, excepting what are known commercially as tin plates, terne plates, and taggers tin, and hereinafter provided for, when galvanized or coated with zinc, spelter, or other metals, or any alloy of those metals, shall pay two-tenths of one cent per pound more duty than if the same was not so galvanized or coated.

133. Sheets of iron or steel, polished, planished, or glanced, by whatever name designated, two cents per pound: *Provided*, That plates or sheets of iron or steel, by whatever name designated, other than the polished, planished, or glanced herein provided for, which have been pickled or cleaned by acid, or by any other material or process, or which

are cold-rolled, smoothed only, not polished, shall pay two-tenths of one cent per pound more duty than the corresponding gauges of common or black sheet iron or steel.

134. Sheets or plates of iron or steel, or taggers iron or steel, coated with tin or lead, or with a mixture of which these metals, or either of them, is a component part, by the dipping or any other process, and commercially known as tin plates, terne plates, and taggers tin, one and one-half cents per pound.

135. Steel ingots, cogged ingots, blooms, and slabs, by whatever process made; die blocks or blanks; billets and bars and tapered or beveled bars; mill shafting; pressed, sheared, or stamped shapes; saw plates, wholly or partially manufactured; hammer molds or swaged steel; gun-barrel molds not in bars; alloys used as substitutes for steel in the manufacture of tools; all descriptions and shapes of dry sand, loam, or iron-molded steel castings; sheets and plates and steel in all forms and shapes not specially provided for in this Act, all of the above valued at one cent per pound or less, three-tenths of one cent per pound; valued above one cent and not above one and four-tenths cents per pound, four-tenths of one cent per pound; valued above one and four-tenths cents and not above one and eight-tenths cents per pound, six-tenths of one cent per pound; valued above one and eight-tenths cents and not above two and two-tenths cents per pound, seven-tenths of one cent per pound; valued above two and two-tenths cents and not above three cents per pound, nine-tenths of one cent per pound; valued above three cents per pound and not above four cents per pound, one and two-tenths cents per pound; valued above four cents and not above seven cents per pound, one and three-tenths cents per pound; valued above seven cents and not above ten cents per pound, two cents per pound; valued above ten cents and not above thirteen cents per pound, two and four-tenths cents per pound; valued above thirteen cents and not above sixteen cents per pound, two and eight-tenths cents per pound; valued above sixteen cents per pound, four and seven-tenths cents per pound.

WIRE:

136. Wire rods: Rivet, screw, fence, and other iron or steel wire rods, whether round, oval, flat, or square, or in any other shape, and nail rods, in coils or otherwise, valued at four cents or less per pound, four-tenths of one cent per pound; valued over four cents per pound, three-fourths of one cent per pound: *Provided*, That all round iron or steel rods smaller than number six wire gauge shall be classed and dutiable as wire: *Provided further*, That all iron or steel wire rods which have been tempered or treated in any manner or partly manufactured shall pay an additional duty of one-half of one cent per pound.

137. Round iron or steel wire, not smaller than number thirteen wire gauge, one and one-fourth cents per pound; smaller than number thirteen and not smaller than number sixteen wire gauge, one and one-half cents per pound; smaller than number sixteen wire gauge, two cents per pound: *Provided*, That all the foregoing valued at more than four cents per pound shall pay forty per centum ad valorem. Iron or steel or other wire not specially provided for in this Act, including such as is commonly known as hat wire, or bonnet wire, crinoline wire, corset wire, needle wire, piano wire, clock wire, and watch wire, whether flat or otherwise, and corset clasps, corset steels and dress steels, and

sheet steel in strips, twenty-five one-thousandths of an inch thick or thinner, any of the foregoing, whether uncovered or covered with cotton, silk, metal, or other material, valued at more than four cents per pound, forty-five per centum ad valorem: *Provided*, That articles manufactured from iron, steel, brass, or copper wire, shall pay the rate of duty imposed upon the wire used in the manufacture of such articles, and in addition thereto one and one-fourth cents per pound, except that wire rope and wire strand shall pay the maximum rate of duty which would be imposed upon any wire used in the manufacture thereof, and in addition thereto one cent per pound; and on iron or steel wire coated with zinc, tin, or any other metal, two-tenths of one cent per pound in addition to the rate imposed on the wire from which it is made.

GENERAL PROVISIONS.

138. No allowance or reduction of duties for partial loss or damage in consequence of rust or of discoloration shall be made upon any description of iron or steel, or upon any article wholly or partly manufactured of iron or steel, or upon any manufacture of iron or steel.

139. All metal produced from iron or its ores, which is cast and malleable, of whatever description or form, without regard to the percentage of carbon contained therein, whether produced by cementation, or converted, cast, or made from iron or its ores, by the crucible, Bessemer, Clapp-Griffith, pneumatic, Thomas-Gilchrist, basic, Siemens-Martin, or open-hearth process, or by the equivalent of either, or by a combination of two or more of the processes, or their equivalents, or by any fusion or other process which produces from iron or its ores a metal either granular or fibrous in structure, which is cast and malleable, excepting what is known as malleable-iron castings, shall be classed and denominated as steel.

140. No article not specially provided for in this Act, which is wholly or partly manufactured from tin plate, terne plate, or the sheet, plate, hoop, band, or scroll iron or steel herein provided for, or of which such tin plate, terne plate, sheet, plate, hoop, band, or scroll iron or steel shall be the material of chief value, shall pay a lower rate of duty than that imposed on the tin plate, terne plate, or sheet, plate, hoop, band, or scroll iron or steel from which it is made, or of which it shall be the component thereof of chief value.

141. On all iron or steel bars or rods of whatever shape or section which are cold rolled, cold drawn, cold hammered, or polished in any way in addition to the ordinary process of hot rolling or hammering, there shall be paid one-fourth of one cent per pound in addition to the rates provided in this Act on bars or rods of whatever section or shape which are hot rolled; and on all strips, plates, or sheets of iron or steel of whatever shape, other than the polished, planished, or glanced sheet-iron or sheet-steel hereinbefore provided for, which are cold rolled, cold hammered, blued, brightened, tempered, or polished by any process to such perfected surface finish or polish better than the grade of cold rolled, smoothed only, hereinbefore provided for, there shall be paid one cent per pound in addition to the rates provided in this Act upon plates, strips, or sheets of iron or steel of common or black finish; and on steel circular saw plates there shall be paid one-half of one cent per pound in addition to the rate provided in this Act for steel saw plates.

14

MANUFACTURES OF IRON AND STEEL.

142. Anvils of iron or steel, or of iron and steel combined, by whatever process made, or in whatever stage of manufacture, one and seven-eighths cents per pound.

143. Axles, or parts thereof, axle bars, axle blanks, or forgings for axles, whether of iron or steel, without reference to the stage or state of manufacture, valued at not more than six cents per pound, one cent per pound: *Provided*, That when iron or steel axles are imported fitted in wheels, or parts of wheels, of iron or steel, they shall be dutiable at the same rate as the wheels in which they are fitted.

144. Blacksmiths' hammers and sledges, track tools, wedges, and crowbars, whether of iron or steel, one and one-half cents per pound.

145. Bolts, with or without threads or nuts, or bolt-blanks, and finished hinges or hinge-blanks, whether of iron or steel, one and one-half cents per pound.

146. Card-clothing manufactured from tempered steel wire, forty-five cents per square foot; all other, twenty cents per square foot.

147. Cast-iron pipe of every description, four-tenths of one cent per pound.

148. Cast-iron vessels, plates, stove-plates, andirons, sad-irons, tailors' irons, hatters' irons, and castings of iron, not specially provided for in this Act, eight-tenths of one cent per pound.

149. Castings of malleable iron not specially provided for in this Act, nine-tenths of one cent per pound.

150. Cast hollow-ware, coated, glazed, or tinned, two cents per pound.

151. Chain or chains of all kinds, made of iron or steel, not less than three-fourths of one inch in diameter, one and one-eighth cents per pound; less than three-fourths of one inch and not less than three-eighths of one inch in diameter, one and three-eighths cents per pound; less than three-eighths of one inch in diameter and not less than five-sixteenths of one inch in diameter, one and seven-eighths cents per pound; less than five-sixteenths of one inch in diameter, three cents per pound; but no chain or chains of any description shall pay a lower rate of duty than forty-five per centum ad valorem.

152. Lap welded, butt welded, seamed, or jointed iron or steel boiler tubes, pipes, flues, or stays, not thinner than number sixteen wire gauge, two cents per pound; welded cylindrical furnaces, made from plate metal, two and one-half cents per pound; all other iron or steel tubes, finished, not specially provided for in this Act, thirty-five per centum ad valorem.

CUTLERY:

153. Penknives or pocketknives, clasp knives, pruning knives, and budding knives of all kinds, or parts thereof, and erasers or manicure knives, or parts thereof, wholly or partly manufactured, valued at not more than forty cents per dozen, forty per centum ad valorem; valued at more than forty cents per dozen and not exceeding fifty cents per dozen, one cent per piece and forty per centum ad valorem; valued at more than fifty cents per dozen and not exceeding one dollar and twenty-five cents per dozen, five cents per piece and forty per centum ad valorem; valued at more than one dollar and twenty-five cents per dozen and not exceeding three dollars per dozen, ten cents per piece and forty per centum ad valorem; valued at more than three dollars per dozen, twenty cents per piece and forty per centum

ad valorem: *Provided*, That blades, handles, or other parts of either or any of the foregoing articles, imported in any other manner than assembled in finished knives or erasers, shall be subject to no less rate of duty than herein provided for penknives, pocketknives, clasp knives, pruning-knives, manicure knives, and erasers valued at more than fifty and not more than one dollar and fifty cents per dozen. Razors and razor blades, finished or unfinished, valued at less than one dollar and fifty cents per dozen, fifty cents per dozen and fifteen per centum ad valorem; valued at one dollar and fifty cents per dozen and less than three dollars per dozen, one dollar per dozen and fifteen per centum ad valorem; valued at three dollars per dozen or more, one dollar and seventy-five cents per dozen and twenty per centum ad valorem. Scissors and shears, and blades for the same, finished or unfinished, valued at not more than fifty cents per dozen, fifteen cents per dozen and fifteen per centum ad valorem; valued at more than fifty cents and not more than one dollar and seventy-five cents per dozen, fifty cents per dozen and fifteen per centum ad valorem; valued at more than one dollar and seventy-five cents per dozen, seventy-five cents per dozen and twenty-five per centum ad valorem.

154. Swords, sword-blades, and side-arms, thirty-five per centum ad valorem.

155. Table, butchers', carving, cooks', hunting, kitchen, bread, butter, vegetable, fruit, cheese, plumbers', painters', palette, artists', and shoe knives, forks and steels, finished or unfinished, with handles of mother-of-pearl, shell or ivory, sixteen cents each; with handles of deer horn, twelve cents each; with handles of hard rubber, solid bone, celluloid or any pyroxyline material, five cents each; with handles of any other material than those above mentioned, one and one-half cents each, and in addition, on all the above articles, fifteen per centum ad valorem: *Provided*, That none of the above-named articles shall pay a less rate of duty than forty-five per centum ad valorem.

156. Files, file-blanks, rasps, and floats, of all cuts and kinds, two and one-half inches in length and under, thirty cents per dozen; over two and one-half inches in length and not over four and one-half inches, fifty cents per dozen; over four and one-half inches in length and under seven inches, seventy-five cents per dozen; seven inches in length and over, one dollar per dozen.

FIREARMS:

157. Muskets, muzzle-loading shotguns, rifles, and parts thereof, twenty-five per centum ad valorem.

158. Double-barreled, sporting, breech-loading shotguns, combination shotguns and rifles, valued at not more than five dollars, one dollar and fifty cents each and in addition thereto fifteen per centum ad valorem; valued at more than five dollars and not more than ten dollars, four dollars each and in addition thereto fifteen per centum ad valorem each; valued at more than ten dollars, six dollars each; double barrels for sporting breech-loading shotguns and rifles further advanced in manufacture than rough bored only, three dollars each; stocks for double-barreled sporting breech-loading shotguns and rifles wholly or partially manu-

factured, three dollars each; and in addition thereto on all such guns and rifles, valued at more than ten dollars each, and on such stocks and barrels, thirty-five per centum ad valorem; on all other parts of such guns or rifles, and fittings for such stocks or barrels, finished or unfinished, fifty per centum ad valorem: *Provided*, That all double-barrel sporting breech-loading shotguns and rifles imported without a lock or locks or other fittings shall be subject to a duty of six dollars each and thirty-five per centum ad valorem; single-barreled breech-loading shotguns, or parts thereof, except as otherwise specially provided for in this Act, one dollar each and thirty-five per centum ad valorem. Revolving pistols or parts thereof, seventy-five cents each and twenty-five per centum ad valorem.

159. Sheets, plates, wares, or articles of iron, steel, or other metal, enameled or glazed with vitreous glasses, forty per centum ad valorem.

NAILS, SPIKES, TACKS, AND NEEDLES:

160. Cut nails and cut spikes of iron or steel, six-tenths of one cent per pound.

161. Horseshoe nails, hob nails, and all other wrought iron or steel nails not specially provided for in this Act, two and one-fourth cents per pound.

162. Wire nails made of wrought iron or steel, not less than one inch in length and not lighter than number sixteen wire gauge, one-half of one cent per pound; less than one inch in length and lighter than number sixteen wire gauge, one cent per pound.

163. Spikes, nuts, and washers, and horse, mule, or ox shoes, of wrought iron or steel, one cent per pound.

164. Cut tacks, brads, or sprigs, not exceeding sixteen ounces to the thousand, one and one-fourth cents per thousand; exceeding sixteen ounces to the thousand, one and one-half cents per pound.

165. Needles for knitting or sewing machines, including latch needles, one dollar per thousand and twenty-five per centum ad valorem; crochet needles and tape needles, knitting and all other needles, not specially provided for in this Act, and bodkins of metal, twenty-five per centum ad valorem.

PLATES:

166. Steel plates engraved, stereotype plates, electrotype plates, and plates of other materials, engraved or lithographed, for printing, twenty-five per centum ad valorem.

167. Rivets of iron or steel, two cents per pound.

SAWS:

168. Crosscut saws, six cents per linear foot; mill saws, ten cents per linear foot; pit, and drag saws, eight cents per linear foot; circular saws, twenty-five per centum ad valorem; steel band saws, finished or further advanced than tempered and polished, ten cents per pound and twenty per centum ad valorem; hand, back, and all other saws, not specially provided for in this Act, thirty per centum ad valorem.

169. Screws, commonly called wood screws, made of iron or steel, more than two inches in length, four cents per pound; over one inch and not more than two inches in length, six cents per pound; over one-half inch and not more than one inch in length, eight and one-half cents per pound; one-half inch and less in length, twelve cents per pound.

170. Umbrella and parasol ribs and stretchers, composed in chief value of iron, steel, or other metal, in frames or otherwise, fifty per centum ad valorem.

171. Wheels for railway purposes, or parts thereof, made of iron or steel, and steel-tired wheels for railway purposes, whether wholly or partly finished, and iron or steel locomotive, car, or other railway tires or parts thereof, wholly or partly manufactured, one and one-half cents per pound; and ingots, cogged ingots, blooms, or blanks for the same, without regard to the degree of manufacture, one and one-fourth cents per pound: *Provided*, That when wheels for railway purposes, or parts thereof, of iron or steel, are imported with iron or steel axles fitted in them, the wheels and axles together shall be dutiable at the same rate as is provided for the wheels when imported separately.

MISCELLANEOUS METALS AND MANUFACTURES OF.

172. Aluminum, and alloys of any kind in which aluminum is the component material of chief value, in crude form, eight cents per pound; in plates, sheets, bars, and rods, thirteen cents per pound.

173. Antimony, as regulus or metal, three-fourths of one cent per pound.

174. Argentine, albata, or German silver, unmanufactured, twenty-five per centum ad valorem.

175. Bronze powder, twelve cents per pound; bronze or Dutch-metal or aluminum, in leaf, six cents per package of one hundred leaves.

176. Copper in rolled plates, called braziers' copper, sheets, rods, pipes, and copper bottoms, two and one-half cents per pound; sheathing or yellow metal of which copper is the component material of chief value, and not composed wholly or in part of iron ungalvanized, two cents per pound.

GOLD AND SILVER:
177. Gold leaf, one dollar and seventy-five cents per package of five hundred leaves.
178. Silver leaf, seventy-five cents per package of five hundred leaves.
179. Tinsel wire, lame or lahn, made wholly or in chief value of gold, silver, or other metal, five cents per pound; bullions and metal threads, made wholly or in chief value of tinsel wire, lame or lahn, five cents per pound and thirty-five per centum ad valorem; laces, embroideries, braids, galloons, trimmings, or other articles, made wholly or in chief value of tinsel wire, lame or lahn, bullions, or metal threads, sixty per centum ad valorem.

180. Hooks and eyes, metallic, whether loose, carded or otherwise, including weight of cards, cartons, and immediate wrappings and labels, five and one-half cents per pound and fifteen per centum ad valorem.

LEAD:
181. Lead-bearing ore of all kinds, one and one-half cents per pound on the lead contained therein: *Provided*, That on all importations of lead-bearing ores the duties shall be estimated at the port of entry, and a bond given in double the amount of such estimated duties for the transportation of the ores by common carriers bonded for the transportation of appraised or unappraised merchandise to properly equipped sampling or smelting establishments, whether designated as bonded warehouses or otherwise. On the arrival of the ores at such establishments

they shall be sampled according to commercial methods under the supervision of Government officers, who shall be stationed at such establishments, and who shall submit the samples thus obtained to a Government assayer, designated by the Secretary of the Treasury, who shall make a proper assay of the sample, and report the result to the proper customs officers, and the import entries shall be liquidated thereon, except in case of ores that shall be removed to a bonded warehouse to be refined for exportation as provided by law. And the Secretary of the Treasury is authorized to make all necessary regulations to enforce the provisions of this paragraph.

182. Lead dross, lead bullion or base bullion, lead in pigs and bars, lead in any form not specially provided for in this Act, old refuse lead run into blocks and bars, and old scrap lead fit only to be remanufactured; all the foregoing, two and one-eighth cents per pound; lead in sheets, pipe, shot, glaziers' lead and lead wire, two and one-half cents per pound.

183. Metallic mineral substances in a crude state, and metals unwrought, not specially provided for in this Act, twenty per centum ad valorem; monazite sand and thorite, six cents per pound.

184. Mica, unmanufactured, or rough trimmed only, six cents per pound and twenty per centum ad valorem; mica, cut or trimmed, twelve cents per pound and twenty per centum ad valorem.

185. Nickel, nickel oxide, alloy of any kind in which nickel is a component material of chief value, in pigs, ingots, bars, or sheets, six cents per pound.

186. Pens, metallic, except gold pens, twelve cents per gross.

187. Penholder tips, penholders or parts thereof, and gold pens, twenty-five per centum ad valorem.

188. Pins with solid heads, without ornamentation, including hair, safety, hat, bonnet, and shawl pins; any of the foregoing composed wholly of brass, copper, iron, steel, or other base metal, not plated, and not commonly known as jewelry, thirty-five per centum ad valorem.

189. Quicksilver, seven cents per pound. The flasks, bottles, or other vessels in which quicksilver is imported shall be subject to the same rate of duty as they would be subjected to if imported empty.

190. Type metal, one and one-half cents per pound for the lead contained therein; new types, twenty-five per centum ad valorem.

191. Watch movements, whether imported in cases or not, if having not more than seven jewels, thirty-five cents each; if having more than seven jewels and not more than eleven jewels, fifty cents each; if having more than eleven jewels and not more than fifteen jewels, seventy-five cents each; if having more than fifteen jewels and not more than seventeen jewels, one dollar and twenty-five cents each; if having more than seventeen jewels, three dollars each, and in addition thereto, on all the foregoing, twenty-five per centum ad valorem; watch cases and parts of watches, including watch dials, chronometers, box or ship, and parts thereof, clocks and parts thereof, not otherwise provided for in this Act, whether separately packed or otherwise, not composed wholly or in part of china, porcelain, parian, bisque or earthenware, forty per centum ad valorem; all jewels for use in the manufacture of watches or clocks, ten per centum ad valorem.

192. Zinc in blocks or pigs, one and one-half cents per pound; in sheets, two cents per pound; old and worn-out, fit only to be remanufactured, one cent per pound.

193. Articles or wares not specially provided for in this Act, composed

wholly or in part of iron, steel, lead, copper, nickel, pewter, zinc, gold, silver, platinum, aluminum or other metal, and whether partly or wholly manufactured, forty-five per centum ad valorem.

SCHEDULE D.—WOOD AND MANUFACTURES OF.

194. Timber hewn, sided, or squared (not less than eight inches square), and round timber used for spars or in building wharves, one cent per cubic foot.

195. Sawed boards, planks, deals, and other lumber of whitewood, sycamore, and basswood, one dollar per thousand feet board measure; sawed lumber, not specially provided for in this Act, two dollars per thousand feet board measure; but when lumber of any sort is planed or finished, in addition to the rates herein provided, there shall be levied and paid for each side so planed or finished fifty cents per thousand feet board measure; and if planed on one side and tongued and grooved, one dollar per thousand feet board measure; and if planed on two sides and tongued and grooved, one dollar and fifty cents per thousand feet board measure; and in estimating board measure under this schedule no deduction shall be made on board measure on account of planing, tongueing and grooving: *Provided*, That if any country or dependency shall impose an export duty upon saw logs, round unmanufactured timber, stave bolts, shingle bolts, or heading bolts, exported to the United States, or a discriminating charge upon boom sticks, or chains used by American citizens in towing logs, the amount of such export duty, tax, or other charge, as the case may be, shall be added as an additional duty to the duties imposed upon the articles mentioned in this paragraph when imported from such country or dependency.

196. Paving posts, railroad ties, and telephone, trolley, electric-light and telegraph poles of cedar or other woods, twenty per centum ad valorem.

197. Kindling wood in bundles not exceeding one-quarter of a cubic foot each, three-tenths of one cent per bundle; if in larger bundles, three-tenths of one cent for each additional quarter of a cubic foot or fractional part thereof.

198. Sawed boards, planks, deals, and all forms of sawed cedar, lignum-vitæ, lancewood, ebony, box, granadilla, mahogany, rosewood, satinwood, and all other cabinet woods not further manufactured than sawed, fifteen per centum ad valorem; veneers of wood, and wood, unmanufactured, not specially provided for in this Act, twenty per centum ad valorem.

199. Clapboards, one dollar and fifty cents per thousand.

200. Hubs for wheels, posts, heading bolts, stave bolts, last-blocks, wagon-blocks, oar-blocks, heading-blocks, and all like blocks or sticks, rough-hewn, sawed or bored, twenty per centum ad valorem; fence posts, ten per centum ad valorem.

201. Laths, twenty-five cents per one thousand pieces.

202. Pickets, palings and staves of wood, of all kinds, ten per centum ad valorem.

203. Shingles, thirty cents per thousand.

204. Casks, barrels, and hogsheads, (empty), sugar-box shooks, and packing-boxes (empty), and packing-box shooks, of wood, not specially provided for in this Act, thirty per centum ad valorem.

205. Boxes, barrels, or other articles containing oranges, lemons, limes, grape fruit, shaddocks or pomelos, thirty per centum ad valorem: *Provided*, That the thin wood, so called, comprising the sides, tops and

bottoms of orange and lemon boxes of the growth and manufacture of the United States, exported as orange and lemon box shooks, may be reimported in completed form, filled with oranges and lemons, by the payment of duty at one-half the rate imposed on similar boxes of entirely foreign growth and manufacture.

206. Chair cane or reeds, wrought or manufactured from rattans or reeds, ten per centum ad valorem; osier or willow prepared for basket makers' use, twenty per centum ad valorem; manufactures of osier or willow, forty per centum ad valorem.

207. Toothpicks of wood or other vegetable substance, two cents per one thousand and fifteen per centum ad valorem; butchers' and packers' skewers of wood, forty cents per thousand.

208. House or cabinet furniture, of wood, wholly or partly finished, and manufactures of wood, or of which wood is the component material of chief value, not specially provided for in this Act, thirty-five per centum ad valorem.

SCHEDULE E.—SUGAR, MOLASSES, AND MANUFACTURES OF.

209. Sugars not above number sixteen Dutch standard in color, tank bottoms, sirups of cane juice, melada, concentrated melada, concrete and concentrated molasses, testing by the polariscope not above seventy-five degrees, ninety-five one-hundredths of one cent per pound, and for every additional degree shown by the polariscopic test, thirty-five one-thousandths of one cent per pound additional, and fractions of a degree in proportion; and on sugar above number sixteen Dutch standard in color, and on all sugar which has gone through a process of refining, one cent and ninety-five one-hundredths of one cent per pound; molasses testing above forty degrees and not above fifty-six degrees, three cents per gallon; testing fifty-six degrees and above, six cents per gallon; sugar drainings and sugar sweepings shall be subject to duty as molasses or sugar, as the case may be, according to polariscopic test: *Provided*, That nothing herein contained shall be so construed as to abrogate or in any manner impair or affect the provisions of the treaty of commercial reciprocity concluded between the United States and the King of the Hawaiian Islands on the thirtieth day of January, eighteen hundred and seventy-five, or the provisions of any Act of Congress heretofore passed for the execution of the same.

210. Maple sugar and maple sirup, four cents per pound; glucose or grape sugar, one and one-half cents per pound; sugar cane in its natural state, or unmanufactured, twenty per centum ad valorem.

211. Saccharine, one dollar and fifty cents per pound and ten per centum ad valorem.

212. Sugar candy and all confectionery not specially provided for in this Act, valued at fifteen cents per pound or less, and on sugars after being refined, when tinctured, colored or in any way adulterated, four cents per pound and fifteen per centum ad valorem; valued at more than fifteen cents per pound, fifty per centum ad valorem. The weight and the value of the immediate coverings, other than the outer packing case or other covering, shall be included in the dutiable weight and the value of the merchandise.

SCHEDULE F.—TOBACCO AND MANUFACTURES OF.

213. Wrapper tobacco, and filler tobacco when mixed or packed with more than fifteen per centum of wrapper tobacco, and all leaf tobacco

the product of two or more countries or dependencies when mixed or packed together, if unstemmed, one dollar and eighty-five cents per pound; if stemmed, two dollars and fifty cents per pound; filler tobacco not specially provided for in this Act, if unstemmed, thirty-five cents per pound; if stemmed, fifty cents per pound.

214. The term wrapper tobacco as used in this Act means that quality of leaf tobacco which is suitable for cigar wrappers, and the term filler tobacco means all other leaf tobacco. Collectors of customs shall not permit entry to be made, except under regulations to be prescribed by the Secretary of the Treasury, of any leaf tobacco, unless the invoices of the same shall specify in detail the character of such tobacco, whether wrapper or filler, its origin and quality. In the examination for classification of any imported leaf tobacco, at least one bale, box, or package in every ten, and at least one in every invoice, shall be examined by the appraiser or person authorized by law to make such examination, and at least ten hands shall be examined in each examined bale, box, or package.

215. All other tobacco, manufactured or unmanufactured, not specially provided for in this Act, fifty-five cents per pound.

216. Snuff and snuff flour, manufactured of tobacco, ground dry, or damp, and pickled, scented, or otherwise, of all descriptions, fifty-five cents per pound.

217. Cigars, cigarettes, cheroots of all kinds, four dollars and fifty cents per pound and twenty-five per centum ad valorem; and paper cigars and cigarettes, including wrappers, shall be subject to the same duties as are herein imposed upon cigars.

SCHEDULE G.—AGRICULTURAL PRODUCTS AND PROVISIONS.

ANIMALS, LIVE:
218. Cattle, if less than one year old, two dollars per head; all other cattle if valued at not more than fourteen dollars per head, three dollars and seventy-five cents per head; if valued at more than fourteen dollars per head, twenty-seven and one-half per centum ad valorem.
219. Swine, one dollar and fifty cents per head.
220. Horses and mules, valued at one hundred and fifty dollars or less per head, thirty dollars per head; if valued at over one hundred and fifty dollars, twenty-five per centum ad valorem.
221. Sheep, one year old or over, one dollar and fifty cents per head; less than one year old, seventy-five cents per head.
222. All other live animals, not specially provided for in this Act, twenty per centum ad valorem.

BREADSTUFFS AND FARINACEOUS SUBSTANCES:
223. Barley, thirty cents per bushel of forty-eight pounds.
224. Barley-malt, forty-five cents per bushel of thirty-four pounds.
225. Barley, pearled, patent, or hulled, two cents per pound.
226. Buckwheat, fifteen cents per bushel of forty-eight pounds.
227. Corn or maize, fifteen cents per bushel of fifty-six pounds.
228. Corn meal, twenty cents per bushel of forty-eight pounds.
229. Macaroni, vermicelli, and all similar preparations, one and one-half cents per pound.
230. Oats, fifteen cents per bushel.
231. Oatmeal and rolled oats, one cent per pound; oat hulls, ten cents per hundred pounds.

232. Rice, cleaned, two cents per pound; uncleaned rice, or rice free of the outer hull and still having the inner cuticle on, one and one-fourth cents per pound; rice flour, and rice meal, and rice broken which will pass through a sieve known commercially as number twelve wire sieve, one-fourth of one cent per pound; paddy, or rice having the outer hull on, three-fourths of one cent per pound.

233. Rye, ten cents per bushel; rye flour, one-half of one cent per pound.

234. Wheat, twenty-five cents per bushel.

235. Wheat flour, twenty-five per centum ad valorem.

DAIRY PRODUCTS:

236. Butter, and substitutes therefor, six cents per pound.

237. Cheese, and substitutes therefor, six cents per pound.

238. Milk, fresh, two cents per gallon.

239. Milk, preserved or condensed, or sterilized by heating or other processes, including weight of immediate coverings, two cents per pound; sugar of milk, five cents per pound.

FARM AND FIELD PRODUCTS:

240. Beans, forty-five cents per bushel of sixty pounds.

241. Beans, pease, and mushrooms, prepared or preserved, in tins, jars, bottles, or similar packages, two and one-half cents per pound, including the weight of all tins, jars, and other immediate coverings; all vegetables, prepared or preserved, including pickles and sauces of all kinds, not specially provided for in this Act, and fish paste or sauce, forty per centum ad valorem.

242. Cabbages, three cents each.

243. Cider, five cents per gallon.

244. Eggs, not specially provided for in this Act, five cents per dozen.

245. Eggs, yolk of, twenty-five per centum ad valorem; albumen, egg or blood, three cents per pound; dried blood, when soluble, one and one-half cents per pound.

246. Hay, four dollars per ton.

247. Honey, twenty cents per gallon.

248. Hops, twelve cents per pound; hop extract and lupulin, fifty per centum ad valorem.

249. Onions, forty cents per bushel; garlic, one cent per pound.

250. Pease, green, in bulk or in barrels, sacks, or similar packages, and seed pease, forty cents per bushel of sixty pounds; pease, dried, not specially provided for, thirty cents per bushel; split pease, forty cents per bushel of sixty pounds; pease in cartons, papers, or other small packages, one cent per pound.

251. Orchids, palms, dracænas, crotons and azaleas, tulips, hyacinths, narcissi, jonquils, lilies, lilies of the valley, and all other bulbs, bulbous roots, or corms, which are cultivated for their flowers, and natural flowers of all kinds, preserved or fresh, suitable for decorative purposes, twenty-five per centum ad valorem.

252. Stocks, cuttings or seedlings of Myrobolan plum, Mahaleb or Mazzard cherry, three years old or less, fifty cents per thousand plants and fifteen per centum ad valorem; stocks, cuttings or seedlings of pear, apple, quince and the St. Julien plum, three years old or less, and evergreen seedlings, one dollar per thousand plants and fifteen per centum ad valorem;

rose plants, budded, grafted, or grown on their own roots, two and one-half cents each; stocks, cuttings and seedlings of all fruit and ornamental trees, deciduous and evergreen, shrubs and vines, manetti, multiflora, and brier rose, and all trees, shrubs, plants and vines, commonly known as nursery or greenhouse stock, not specially provided for in this Act, twenty-five per centum ad valorem.

253. Potatoes, twenty-five cents per bushel of sixty pounds.

254. Seeds: Castor beans or seeds, twenty-five cents per bushel of fifty pounds; flaxseed or linseed and other oil seeds not specially provided for in this Act, twenty-five cents per bushel of fifty-six pounds; poppy seed, fifteen cents per bushel; but no drawback shall be allowed upon oil cake made from imported seed, nor shall any allowance be made for dirt or other impurities in any seed; seeds of all kinds not specially provided for in this Act, thirty per centum ad valorem.

255. Straw, one dollar and fifty cents per ton.

256. Teazles, thirty per centum ad valorem.

257. Vegetables in their natural state, not specially provided for in this Act, twenty-five per centum ad valorem.

FISH:

258. Fish known or labeled as anchovies, sardines, sprats, brislings, sardels, or sardellen, packed in oil or otherwise, in bottles, jars, tin boxes or cans, shall be dutiable as follows: When in packages containing seven and one-half cubic inches or less, one and one-half cents per bottle, jar, box or can; containing more than seven and one-half and not more than twenty-one cubic inches, two and one-half cents per bottle, jar, box or can; containing more than twenty-one and not more than thirty-three cubic inches, five cents per bottle, jar, box or can; containing more than thirty-three and not more than seventy cubic inches, ten cents per bottle, jar, box or can; if in other packages, forty per centum ad valorem. All other fish, (except shellfish), in tin packages, thirty per centum ad valorem; fish in packages containing less than one-half barrel, and not specially provided for in this Act, thirty per centum ad valorem.

259. Fresh-water fish not specially provided for in this Act, one-fourth of one cent per pound.

260. Herrings, pickled or salted, one-half of one cent per pound; herrings, fresh, one-fourth of one cent per pound.

261. Fish, fresh, smoked, dried, salted, pickled, frozen, packed in ice or otherwise prepared for preservation, not specially provided for in this Act, three-fourths of one cent per pound; fish, skinned or boned, one and one-fourth cents per pound; mackerel, halibut or salmon, fresh, pickled or salted, one cent per pound.

FRUITS AND NUTS:

262. Apples, peaches, quinces, cherries, plums, and pears, green or ripe, twenty-five cents per bushel; apples, peaches, pears, and other edible fruits, including berries, when dried, desiccated, evaporated or prepared in any manner, not specially provided for in this Act, two cents per pound; berries, edible, in their natural condition, one cent per quart; cranberries, twenty-five per centum ad valorem.

263. Comfits, sweetmeats, and fruits preserved in sugar, molasses, spirits, or in their own juices, not specially provided for in this

Act, one cent per pound and thirty-five per centum ad valorem; if containing over ten per centum of alcohol and not specially provided for in this Act, thirty-five per centum ad valorem and in addition two dollars and fifty cents per proof gallon on the alcohol contained therein in excess of ten per centum; jellies of all kinds, thirty-five per centum ad valorem; pineapples preserved in their own juice, twenty-five per centum ad valorem.

264. Figs, plums, prunes, and prunelles, two cents per pound; raisins and other dried grapes, two and one-half cents per pound; dates, one-half of one cent per pound; currants, Zante or other, two cents per pound; olives, green or prepared, in bottles, jars, or similar packages, twenty-five cents per gallon; in casks or otherwise than in bottles, jars, or similar packages, fifteen cents per gallon.

265. Grapes in barrels or other packages, twenty cents per cubic foot of capacity of barrels or packages.

266. Oranges, lemons, limes, grape fruit, shaddocks or pomelos, one cent per pound.

267. Orange peel or lemon peel, preserved, candied, or dried, and cocoanut meat or copra desiccated, shredded, cut, or similarly prepared, two cents per pound; citron or citron peel, preserved, candied, or dried, four cents per pound.

268. Pineapples, in barrels and other packages, seven cents per cubic foot of the capacity of barrels or packages; in bulk, seven dollars per thousand.

Nuts—

269. Almonds, not shelled, four cents per pound; clear almonds, shelled, six cents per pound.

270. Filberts and walnuts of all kinds, not shelled, three cents per pound; shelled, five cents per pound.

271. Peanuts or ground beans, unshelled, one-half of one cent per pound; shelled, one cent per pound.

272. Nuts of all kinds, shelled or unshelled, not specially provided for in this Act, one cent per pound.

MEAT PRODUCTS:

273. Bacon and hams, five cents per pound.

274. Fresh beef, veal, mutton, and pork, two cents per pound.

275. Meats of all kinds, prepared or preserved, not specially provided for in this Act, twenty-five per centum ad valorem.

276. Extract of meat, not specially provided for in this Act, thirty-five cents per pound; fluid extract of meat, fifteen cents per pound, but the dutiable weight of the extract of meat and of the fluid extract of meat shall not include the weight of the package in which the same is imported.

277. Lard, two cents per pound.

278. Poultry, live, three cents per pound; dressed, five cents per pound.

279. Tallow, three-fourths of one cent per pound; wool grease, including that known commercially as degras or brown wool grease, one-half of one cent per pound.

MISCELLANEOUS PRODUCTS:

280. Chicory-root, raw, dried, or undried, but unground, one cent per pound; chicory root, burnt or roasted, ground or granulated, or in rolls, or otherwise prepared, and not specially provided for in this Act, two and one-half cents per pound.

281. Chocolate and cocoa, prepared or manufactured, not specially provided for in this Act, valued at not over fifteen cents per pound, two and one-half cents per pound; valued above fifteen and not above twenty-four cents per pound, two and one-half cents per pound and ten per centum ad valorem; valued above twenty-four and not above thirty-five cents per pound, five cents per pound and ten per centum ad valorem; valued above thirty-five cents per pound, fifty per centum ad valorem. The weight and value of all coverings, other than plain wooden, shall be included in the dutiable weight and value of the foregoing merchandise; powdered cocoa, unsweetened, five cents per pound.

282. Cocoa-butter or cocoa-butterine, three and one-half cents per pound.

283. Dandelion-root and acorns prepared, and articles used as coffee, or as substitutes for coffee not specially provided for in this Act, two and one-half cents per pound.

284. Salt in bags, sacks, barrels, or other packages, twelve cents per one hundred pounds; in bulk, eight cents per one hundred pounds: *Provided*, That imported salt in bond may be used in curing fish taken by vessels licensed to engage in the fisheries, and in curing fish on the shores of the navigable waters of the United States, under such regulations as the Secretary of the Treasury shall prescribe; and upon proof that the salt has been used for either of the purposes stated in this proviso, the duties on the same shall be remitted: *Provided further*, That exporters of meats, whether packed or smoked, which have been cured in the United States with imported salt, shall, upon satisfactory proof, under such regulations as the Secretary of the Treasury shall prescribe, that such meats have been cured with imported salt, have refunded to them from the Treasury the duties paid on the salt so used in curing such exported meats, in amounts not less than one hundred dollars.

285. Starch, including all preparations, from whatever substance produced, fit for use as starch, one and one-half cents per pound.

286. Dextrine, burnt starch, gum substitute, or British gum, two cents per pound.

287. Spices: Mustard, ground or prepared, in bottles or otherwise, ten cents per pound; capsicum or red pepper, or cayenne pepper, two and one-half cents per pound; sage, one cent per pound; spices not specially provided for in this Act, three cents per pound.

288. Vinegar, seven and one-half cents per proof gallon. The standard proof for vinegar shall be taken to be that strength which requires thirty-five grains of bicarbonate of potash to neutralize one ounce troy of vinegar.

SCHEDULE H.—SPIRITS, WINES, AND OTHER BEVERAGES.

SPIRITS.

289. Brandy and other spirits manufactured or distilled from grain or other materials, and not specially provided for in this Act, two dollars and twenty-five cents per proof gallon.

290. Each and every gauge or wine gallon of measurement shall be counted as at least one proof gallon; and the standard for determining

the proof of brandy and other spirits or liquors of any kind imported shall be the same as that which is defined in the laws relating to internal revenue: *Provided*, That it shall be lawful for the Secretary of the Treasury, in his discretion, to authorize the ascertainment of the proof of wines, cordials, or other liquors, by distillation or otherwise, in cases where it is impracticable to ascertain such proof by the means prescribed by existing law or regulations: *And provided further*, That any brandy or other spirituous or distilled liquors imported in any sized cask, bottle, jug, or other package, of or from any country, dependency, or province under whose laws similar sized casks, bottles, jugs, or other packages of distilled spirits, wine, or other beverage put up or filled in the United States are denied entrance into such country, dependency, or province, shall be forfeited to the United States; and any brandy or other spirituous or distilled liquor imported in a cask of less capacity than ten gallons from any country shall be forfeited to the United States.

291. On all compounds or preparations of which distilled spirits are a component part of chief value, there shall be levied a duty not less than that imposed upon distilled spirits.

292. Cordials, liqueurs, arrack, absinthe, kirschwasser, ratafia, and other spirituous beverages or bitters of all kinds, containing spirits, and not specially provided for in this Act, two dollars and twenty-five cents per proof gallon.

293. No lower rate or amount of duty shall be levied, collected, and paid on brandy, spirits, and other spirituous beverages than that fixed by law for the description of first proof; but it shall be increased in proportion for any greater strength than the strength of first proof, and all imitations of brandy or spirits or wines imported by any names whatever shall be subject to the highest rate of duty provided for the genuine articles respectively intended to be represented, and in no case less than one dollar and fifty cents per gallon.

294. Bay rum or bay water, whether distilled or compounded, of first proof, and in proportion for any greater strength than first proof, one dollar and fifty cents per gallon.

WINES.

295. Champagne and all other sparkling wines, in bottles containing each not more than one quart and more than one pint, eight dollars per dozen; containing not more than one pint each and more than one-half pint, four dollars per dozen; containing one-half pint each or less, two dollars per dozen; in bottles or other vessels containing more than one quart each, in addition to eight dollars per dozen bottles, on the quantity in excess of one quart, at the rate of two dollars and fifty cents per gallon; but no separate or additional duty shall be levied on the bottles.

296. Still wines, including ginger wine or ginger cordial and vermuth, in casks or packages other than bottles or jugs, if containing fourteen per centum or less of absolute alcohol, forty cents per gallon; if containing more than fourteen per centum of absolute alcohol, fifty cents per gallon. In bottles or jugs, per case of one dozen bottles or jugs, containing each not more than one quart and more than one pint, or twenty-four bottles or jugs containing each not more than one pint, one dollar and sixty cents per case; and any excess beyond these quantities found in such bottles or jugs shall be subject to a duty of five cents per pint or fractional part thereof, but no separate or additional

duty shall be assessed on the bottles or jugs: *Provided*, That any wines, ginger cordial, or vermuth imported containing more than twenty-four per centum of alcohol shall be classed as spirits and pay duty accordingly: *And provided further*, That there shall be no constructive or other allowance for breakage, leakage, or damage on wines, liquors, cordials, or distilled spirits. Wines, cordials, brandy, and other spirituous liquors, including bitters of all kinds, and bay rum or bay water, imported in bottles or jugs, shall be packed in packages containing not less than one dozen bottles or jugs in each package, or duty shall be paid as if such package contained at least one dozen bottles or jugs, and in addition thereto, duty shall be collected on the bottles or jugs at the rates which would be chargeable thereon if imported empty. The percentage of alcohol in wines and fruit juices shall be determined in such manner as the Secretary of the Treasury shall by regulation prescribe.

297. Ale, porter, and beer, in bottles or jugs, forty cents per gallon, but no separate or additional duty shall be assessed on the bottles or jugs; otherwise than in bottles or jugs, twenty cents per gallon.

298. Malt extract, fluid, in casks, twenty cents per gallon; in bottles or jugs, forty cents per gallon; solid or condensed, forty per centum ad valorem.

299. Cherry juice and prune juice, or prune wine, and other fruit juices not specially provided for in this Act, containing no alcohol or not more than eighteen per centum of alcohol, sixty cents per gallon; if containing more than eighteen per centum of alcohol, sixty cents per gallon, and in addition thereto two dollars and seven cents per proof gallon on the alcohol contained therein.

300. Ginger ale, ginger beer, lemonade, soda water, and other similar beverages containing no alcohol in plain green or colored, molded or pressed, glass bottles, containing each not more than three-fourths of a pint, eighteen cents per dozen; containing more than three-fourths of a pint each and not more than one and one-half pints, twenty-eight cents per dozen; but no separate or additional duty shall be assessed on the bottles; if imported otherwise than in plain green or colored, molded or pressed, glass bottles, or in such bottles containing more than one and one-half pints each, fifty cents per gallon and in addition thereto, duty shall be collected on the bottles, or other coverings, at the rates which would be chargeable thereon if imported empty.

301. All mineral waters and all imitations of natural mineral waters, and all artificial mineral waters not specially provided for in this Act, in green or colored glass bottles, containing not more than one pint, twenty cents per dozen bottles. If containing more than one pint and not more than one quart, thirty cents per dozen bottles. But no separate duty shall be assessed upon the bottles. If imported otherwise than in plain green or colored glass bottles, or if imported in such bottles containing more than one quart, twenty-four cents per gallon, and in addition thereto duty shall be collected upon the bottles or other covering at the same rates that would be charged thereon if imported empty or separately.

SCHEDULE I.—COTTON MANUFACTURES.

302. Cotton thread and carded yarn, warps or warp yarn, in singles, whether on beams or in bundles, skeins or cops, or in any other form, except spool thread of cotton hereinafter provided for, not colored, bleached, dyed, or advanced beyond the condition of singles by group-

ing or twisting two or more single yarns together, three cents per pound on all numbers up to and including number fifteen, one-fifth of a cent per number per pound on all numbers exceeding number fifteen and up to and including number thirty, and one-fourth of a cent per number per pound on all numbers exceeding number thirty; colored, bleached, dyed, combed or advanced beyond the condition of singles by grouping or twisting two or more single yarns together, whether on beams, or in bundles, skeins or cops, or in any other form, except spool thread of cotton hereinafter provided for, six cents per pound on all numbers up to and including number twenty, and on all numbers exceeding number twenty and up to number eighty, one-fourth of one cent per number per pound; on number eighty and above, three-tenths of one cent per number per pound; cotton card laps, roping, sliver or roving, forty-five per centum ad valorem.

303. Spool thread of cotton, including crochet, darning, and embroidery cottons on spools or reels, containing on each spool or reel not exceeding one hundred yards of thread, six cents per dozen; exceeding one hundred yards on each spool or reel, for every additional hundred yards or fractional part thereof in excess of one hundred, six cents per dozen spools or reels; if otherwise than on spools or reels, one-half of one cent for each one hundred yards or fractional part thereof: *Provided*, That in no case shall the duty be assessed upon a less number of yards than is marked on the spools or reels.

304. Cotton cloth not bleached, dyed, colored, stained, painted, or printed, and not exceeding fifty threads to the square inch, counting the warp and filling, one cent per square yard; if bleached, one and one-fourth cents per square yard; if dyed, colored, stained, painted, or printed, two cents per square yard.

305. Cotton cloth, not bleached, dyed, colored, stained, painted, or printed, exceeding fifty and not exceeding one hundred threads to the square inch, counting the warp and filling, and not exceeding six square yards to the pound, one and one-fourth cents per square yard; exceeding six and not exceeding nine square yards to the pound, one and one-half cents per square yard; exceeding nine square yards to the pound, one and three-fourths cents per square yard; if bleached, and not exceeding six square yards to the pound, one and one-half cents per square yard; exceeding six and not exceeding nine square yards to the pound, one and three-fourths cents per square yard; exceeding nine square yards to the pound, two and one-fourth cents per square yard; if dyed, colored, stained, painted, or printed, and not exceeding six square yards to the pound, two and three-fourths cents per square yard; exceeding six and not exceeding nine square yards to the pound, three and one-fourth cents per square yard; exceeding nine square yards to the pound, three and one-half cents per square yard: *Provided*, That on all cotton cloth not exceeding one hundred threads to the square inch, counting the warp and filling, not bleached, dyed, colored, stained, painted, or printed, valued at over seven cents per square yard, twenty-five per centum ad valorem; bleached, valued at over nine cents per square yard, twenty-five per centum ad valorem; and dyed, colored, stained, painted, or printed, valued at over twelve cents per square yard, there shall be levied, collected, and paid a duty of thirty per centum ad valorem.

306. Cotton cloth, not bleached, dyed, colored, stained, painted, or printed, exceeding one hundred and not exceeding one hundred and fifty threads to the square inch, counting the warp and filling, and not exceeding four square yards to the pound, one and one-half cents per

square yard; exceeding four and not exceeding six square yards to the pound, two cents per square yard; exceeding six and not exceeding eight square yards to the pound, two and one-half cents per square yard; exceeding eight square yards to the pound, two and three-fourths cents per square yard; if bleached, and not exceeding four square yards to the pound, two and one-half cents per square yard; exceeding four and not exceeding six square yards to the pound, three cents per square yard; exceeding six and not exceeding eight square yards to the pound, three and one-half cents per square yard; exceeding eight square yards to the pound, three and three-fourths cents per square yard; if dyed, colored, stained, painted, or printed, and not exceeding four square yards to the pound, three and one-half cents per square yard; exceeding four and not exceeding six square yards to the pound, three and three-fourths cents per square yard; exceeding six and not exceeding eight square yards to the pound, four and one-fourth cents per square yard; exceeding eight square yards to the pound, four and one-half cents per square yard: *Provided*, That on all cotton cloth exceeding one hundred and not exceeding one hundred and fifty threads to the square inch, counting the warp and filling, not bleached, dyed, colored, stained, painted, or printed, valued at over nine cents per square yard, thirty per centum ad valorem; bleached, valued at over eleven cents per square yard, thirty-five per centum ad valorem; dyed, colored, stained, painted, or printed, valued at over twelve and one-half cents per square yard, there shall be levied, collected, and paid a duty of thirty-five per centum ad valorem.

307. Cotton cloth not bleached, dyed, colored, stained, painted, or printed, exceeding one hundred and fifty and not exceeding two hundred threads to the square inch, counting the warp and filling, and not exceeding three and one-half square yards to the pound, two cents per square yard; exceeding three and one-half and not exceeding four and one-half square yards to the pound, two and three-fourths cents per square yard; exceeding four and one-half and not exceeding six square yards to the pound, three cents per square yard; exceeding six square yards to the pound, three and one-half cents per square yard; if bleached, and not exceeding three and one-half square yards to the pound, two and three-fourths cents per square yard; exceeding three and one-half and not exceeding four and one-half square yards to the pound, three and one-half cents per square yard; exceeding four and one-half and not exceeding six square yards to the pound, four cents per square yard; exceeding six square yards to the pound, four and one-fourth cents per square yard; if dyed, colored, stained, painted, or printed, and not exceeding three and one-half square yards to the pound, four and one-fourth cents per square yard; exceeding three and one-half and not exceeding four and one-half square yards to the pound, four and one-half cents per square yard; exceeding four and one-half and not exceeding six square yards to the pound, four and three-fourths cents per square yard; exceeding six square yards to the pound, five cents per square yard: *Provided*, That on all cotton cloth exceeding one hundred and fifty and not exceeding two hundred threads to the square inch, counting the warp and filling, not bleached, dyed, colored, stained, painted, or printed, valued at over ten cents per square yard, thirty-five per centum ad valorem; bleached, valued at over twelve cents per square yard, thirty-five per centum ad volorem; dyed, colored, stained, painted, or printed, valued at over twelve and one-half cents per square yard, there shall be levied, collected, and paid a duty of forty per centum ad valorem.

308. Cotton cloth not bleached, dyed, colored, stained, painted, or printed, exceeding two hundred and not exceeding three hundred threads to the square inch, counting the warp and filling, and not exceeding two and one-half square yards to the pound, three and one-half cents per square yard; exceeding two and one-half and not exceeding three and one-half square yards to the pound, four cents per square yard; exceeding three and one-half and not exceeding five square yards to the pound, four and one-half cents per square yard; exceeding five square yards to the pound, five cents per square yard; if bleached, and not exceeding two and one-half square yards to the pound, four and one-half cents per square yard; exceeding two and one-half and not exceeding three and one-half square yards to the pound, five cents per square yard; exceeding three and one-half and not exceeding five square yards to the pound, five and one-half cents per square yard; exceeding five square yards to the pound, six cents per square yard; if dyed, colored, stained, painted, or printed, and not exceeding three and one-half square yards to the pound, six and one-fourth cents per square yard; exceeding three and one-half square yards to the pound, seven cents per square yard: *Provided*, That on all such cotton cloths not bleached, dyed, colored, stained, painted, or printed, valued at over twelve and one-half cents per square yard; bleached, valued at over fifteen cents per square yard; and dyed, colored, stained, painted, or printed, valued at over seventeen and one-half cents per square yard, there shall be levied, collected, and paid a duty of forty per centum ad valorem.

309. Cotton cloth not bleached, dyed, colored, stained, painted, or printed, exceeding three hundred threads to the square inch, counting the warp and filling, and not exceeding two square yards to the pound, four cents per square yard; exceeding two and not exceeding three square yards to the pound, four and one-half cents per square yard; exceeding three and not exceeding four square yards to the pound, five cents per square yard; exceeding four square yards to the pound, five and one-half cents per square yard; if bleached and not exceeding two square yards to the pound, five cents per square yard; exceeding two and not exceeding three square yards to the pound, five and one-half cents per square yard; exceeding three and not exceeding four square yards to the pound, six cents per square yard; exceeding four square yards to the pound, six and one-half cents per square yard; if dyed, colored, stained, painted, or printed, and not exceeding three square yards to the pound, six and one-half cents per square yard; exceeding three square yards to the pound, eight cents per square yard: *Provided*, That on all such cotton cloths not bleached, dyed, colored, stained, painted, or printed, valued at over fourteen cents per square yard; bleached, valued at over sixteen cents per square yard; and dyed, colored, stained, painted, or printed, valued at over twenty cents per square yard, there shall be levied, collected, and paid a duty of forty per centum ad valorem.

310. The term cotton cloth, or cloth, wherever used in the paragraphs of this schedule, unless otherwise specially provided for, shall be held to include all woven fabrics of cotton in the piece or otherwise, whether figured, fancy, or plain, the warp and filling threads of which can be counted by unraveling or other practicable means.

311. Cloth, composed of cotton or other vegetable fiber and silk, whether known as silk-striped sleeve linings, silk stripes, or otherwise, of which cotton is the component material of chief value, eight cents per square yard and thirty per centum ad valorem: *Provided*, That

no such cloth shall pay a less rate of duty than fifty per centum ad valorem. Cotton cloth, filled or coated, three cents per square yard and twenty per centum ad valorem.

312. Handkerchiefs or mufflers composed of cotton, whether in the piece or otherwise and whether finished or unfinished, if not hemmed, or hemmed only, shall pay the same rate of duty on the cloth contained therein as is imposed on cotton cloth of the same description, weight, and count of threads to the square inch; but such handkerchiefs or mufflers shall not pay a less rate of duty than forty-five per centum ad valorem. If such handkerchiefs or mufflers are hemstitched, or imitation hemstitched, or revered, or have drawn threads, they shall pay a duty of ten per centum ad valorem in addition to the duty hereinbefore prescribed, and in no case less than fifty-five per centum ad valorem; if such handkerchiefs or mufflers are embroidered in any manner, whether with an initial letter, monogram, or otherwise, by hand or machinery, or are tamboured, appliqued, or trimmed wholly or in part with lace or with tucking or insertion, they shall not pay a less rate of duty than sixty per centum ad valorem.

313. Cotton cloth in which other than the ordinary warp and filling threads have been introduced in the process of weaving to form a figure, whether known as lappets or otherwise, and whether unbleached, bleached, dyed, colored, stained, painted, or printed, shall pay, in addition to the duty herein provided for other cotton cloth of the same description, or condition, weight, and count of threads to the square inch, one cent per square yard if valued at not more than seven cents per square yard, and two cents per square yard if valued at more than seven cents per square yard.

314. Clothing, ready-made, and articles of wearing apparel of every description, including neck-ties or neckwear composed of cotton or other vegetable fiber, or of which cotton or other vegetable fiber is the component material of chief value, made up or manufactured, wholly or in part, by the tailor, seamstress, or manufacturer, and not otherwise provided for in this Act, fifty per centum ad valorem: *Provided*, That any outside garment provided for in this paragraph having india-rubber as a component material shall pay a duty of fifteen cents per pound and fifty per centum ad valorem.

315. Plushes, velvets, velveteens, corduroys, and all pile fabrics, cut or uncut; any of the foregoing composed of cotton or other vegetable fiber, not bleached, dyed, colored, stained, painted, or printed, nine cents per square yard and twenty-five per centum ad valorem; if bleached, dyed, colored, stained, painted, or printed, twelve cents per square yard and twenty-five per centum ad valorem: *Provided*, That corduroys composed of cotton or other vegetable fiber, weighing seven ounces or over per square yard, shall pay a duty of eighteen cents per square yard and twenty-five per centum ad valorem: *Provided further*, That manufactures or articles in any form including such as are commonly known as bias dress facings or skirt bindings, made or cut from plushes, velvets, velveteens, corduroys, or other pile fabrics composed of cotton or other vegetable fiber, shall be subject to the foregoing rates of duty and in addition thereto ten per centum ad valorem: *Provided further*, That none of the articles or fabrics provided for in this paragraph shall pay a less rate of duty than forty-seven and one-half per centum ad valorem.

316. Curtains, table covers, and all articles manufactured of cotton chenille or of which cotton chenille is the component material of chief value, fifty per centum ad valorem.

317. Stockings, hose and half-hose, made on knitting machines or frames, composed of cotton or other vegetable fiber, and not otherwise specially provided for in this Act, thirty per centum ad valorem.

318. Stockings, hose and half-hose, selvedged, fashioned, narrowed, or shaped wholly or in part by knitting machines or frames, or knit by hand, including such as are commercially known as seamless stockings, hose and half-hose, and clocked stockings, hose or half-hose, all of the above composed of cotton or other vegetable fiber, finished or unfinished, valued at not more than one dollar per dozen pairs, fifty cents per dozen pairs; valued at more than one dollar per dozen pairs, and not more than one dollar and fifty cents per dozen pairs, sixty cents per dozen pairs; valued at more than one dollar and fifty cents per dozen pairs, and not more than two dollars per dozen pairs, seventy cents per dozen pairs; valued at more than two dollars per dozen pairs, and not more than three dollars per dozen pairs, one dollar and twenty cents per dozen pairs; valued at more than three dollars per dozen pairs and not more than five dollars per dozen pairs, two dollars per dozen pairs; and in addition thereto, upon all the foregoing, fifteen per centum ad valorem; valued at more than five dollars per dozen pairs, fifty-five per centum ad valorem.

319. Shirts and drawers, pants, vests, union suits, combination suits, tights, sweaters, corset covers and all underwear of every description made wholly or in part on knitting machines or frames, or knit by hand, finished or unfinished, not including stockings, hose and half-hose, composed of cotton or other vegetable fiber, valued at not more than one dollar and fifty cents per dozen, sixty cents per dozen and fifteen per centum ad valorem; valued at more than one dollar and fifty cents per dozen and not more than three dollars per dozen, one dollar and ten cents per dozen, and in addition thereto fifteen per centum ad valorem; valued at more than three dollars per dozen and not more than five dollars per dozen, one dollar and fifty cents per dozen, and in addition thereto twenty-five per centum ad valorem; valued at more than five dollars per dozen and not more than seven dollars per dozen, one dollar and seventy-five cents per dozen, and in addition thereto thirty-five per centum ad valorem; valued at more than seven dollars per dozen and not more than fifteen dollars per dozen, two dollars and twenty-five cents per dozen, and in addition thereto thirty-five per centum ad valorem; valued above fifteen dollars per dozen, fifty per centum ad valorem.

320. Bandings, beltings, bindings, bone casings, cords, garters, lining for bicycle tires, ribbons, suspenders and braces, tapes, tubing, and webs or webbing, any of the foregoing articles made of cotton or other vegetable fiber, whether composed in part of india-rubber or otherwise, and not embroidered by hand or machinery, forty-five per centum ad valorem; spindle banding, woven, braided or twisted lamp, stove, or candle wicking made of cotton or other vegetable fiber, ten cents per pound and fifteen per centum ad valorem; loom harness or healds made of cotton or other vegetable fiber, or of which cotton or other vegetable fiber is the component material of chief value, fifty cents per pound and twenty-five per centum ad valorem; boot, shoe, and corset lacings made of cotton or other vegetable fiber, twenty-five cents per pound and fifteen per centum ad valorem; labels, for garments or other articles, composed of cotton or other vegetable fiber, fifty cents per pound and thirty per centum ad valorem.

321. Cotton table damask, forty per centum ad valorem; cotton duck, thirty-five per centum ad valorem.

322. All manufactures of cotton not specially provided for in this Act, forty-five per centum ad valorem.

SCHEDULE J.—FLAX, HEMP, AND JUTE, AND MANUFACTURES OF.

323. Flax straw, five dollars per ton.
324. Flax, not hackled or dressed, one cent per pound.
325. Flax, hackled, known as "dressed line," three cents per pound.
326. Tow of flax, twenty dollars per ton.
327. Hemp, and tow of hemp, twenty dollars per ton; hemp, hackled, known as "line of hemp," forty dollars per ton.
328. Single yarns made of jute, not finer than five lea or number, one cent per pound and ten per centum ad valorem; if finer than five lea or number, thirty-five per centum ad valorem.
329. Cables and cordage, composed of istle, Tampico fiber, manila, sisal grass or sunn, or a mixture of these or any of them, one cent per pound; cables and cordage made of hemp, tarred or untarred, two cents per pound.
330. Threads, twines, or cords, made from yarn not finer than five lea or number, composed of flax, hemp, or ramie, or of which these substances or either of them is the component material of chief value, thirteen cents per pound; if made from yarn finer than five lea or number, three-fourths of one cent per pound additional for each lea or number, or part of a lea or number, in excess of five.
331. Single yarns in the gray, made of flax, hemp, or ramie, or a mixture of any of them, not finer than eight lea or number, seven cents per pound; finer than eight lea or number and not finer than eighty lea or number, forty per centum ad valorem; single yarns, made of flax, hemp, or ramie, or a mixture of any of them, finer than eighty lea or number, fifteen per centum ad valorem.
332. Flax gill netting, nets, webs, and seines shall pay the same duty per pound as is imposed in this schedule upon the thread, twine, or cord of which they are made, and in addition thereto twenty-five per centum ad valorem.
333. Floor mattings, plain, fancy or figured, manufactured from straw, round or split, or other vegetable substances not otherwise provided for, including what are commonly known as Chinese, Japanese, and India straw mattings, valued at not exceeding ten cents per square yard, three cents per square yard; valued at exceeding ten cents per square yard, seven cents per square yard and twenty-five per centum ad valorem.
334. Carpets, carpeting, mats and rugs made of flax, hemp, jute, or other vegetable fiber (except cotton), valued at not exceeding fifteen cents per square yard, five cents per square yard and thirty-five per centum ad valorem; valued above fifteen cents per square yard, ten cents per square yard and thirty-five per centum ad valorem.
335. Hydraulic hose, made in whole or in part of flax, hemp, ramie, or jute, twenty cents per pound.
336. Tapes composed wholly or in part of flax, woven with or without metal threads, on reels, spools, or otherwise, and designed expressly for use in the manufacture of measuring tapes, forty per centum ad valorem.
337. Oilcloth for floors, stamped, painted, or printed, including linoleum or corticene, figured or plain, and all other oilcloth (except silk oilcloth) under twelve feet in width not specially provided for herein, eight cents per square yard and fifteen per centum ad valorem; oil

cloth for floors and linoleum or corticene, twelve feet and over in width, inlaid linoleum or corticene, and cork carpets, twenty cents per square yard and twenty per centum ad valorem; waterproof cloth, composed of cotton or other vegetable fiber, whether composed in part of india-rubber or otherwise, ten cents per square yard and twenty per centum ad valorem.

338. Shirt collars and cuffs, composed of cotton, forty-five cents per dozen pieces and fifteen per centum ad valorem; composed in whole or in part of linen, forty cents per dozen pieces and twenty per centum ad valorem.

339. Laces, lace window curtains, tidies, pillow shams, bed sets, insertings, flouncings, and other lace articles; handkerchiefs, napkins, wearing apparel, and other articles, made wholly or in part of lace, or in imitation of lace; nets or nettings, veils and veilings, etamines, vitrages, neck rufflings, ruchings, tuckings, flutings, and quillings; embroideries and all trimmings, including braids, edgings, insertings, flouncings, galloons, gorings, and bands; wearing apparel, handkerchiefs, and other articles or fabrics embroidered in any manner by hand or machinery, whether with a letter, monogram, or otherwise; tamboured or appliquéed articles, fabrics or wearing apparel; hemstitched or tucked flouncings or skirtings, and articles made wholly or in part of rufflings, tuckings, or ruchings; all of the foregoing, composed wholly or in chief value of flax, cotton, or other vegetable fiber, and not elsewhere specially provided for in this Act, whether composed in part of india rubber or otherwise, sixty per centum ad valorem: *Provided*, That no wearing apparel or other article or textile fabric, when embroidered by hand or machinery, shall pay duty at a less rate than that imposed in any schedule of this Act upon any embroideries of the materials of which such embroidery is composed.

340. Lace window curtains, pillow shams, and bed sets, finished or unfinished, made on the Nottingham lace-curtain machine or on the Nottingham warp machine, and composed of cotton or other vegetable fiber, when counting five points or spaces between the warp threads to the inch, one cent per square yard; when counting more than five such points or spaces to the inch, one-half of one cent per square yard in addition for each such point or space to the inch in excess of five; and in addition thereto, on all the foregoing articles in this paragraph, twenty per centum ad valorem: *Provided*, That none of the above-named articles shall pay a less rate of duty than fifty per centum ad valorem.

341. Plain woven fabrics of single jute yarns, by whatever name known, not exceeding sixty inches in width, weighing not less than six ounces per square yard and not exceeding thirty threads to the square inch, counting the warp and filling, five-eighths of one cent per pound and fifteen per centum ad valorem; if exceeding thirty and not exceeding fifty-five threads to the square inch, counting the warp and filling, seven-eighths of one cent per pound and fifteen per centum ad valorem.

342. All pile fabrics of which flax is the component material of chief value, sixty per centum ad valorem.

343. Bags or sacks made from plain woven fabrics, of single jute yarns, not dyed, colored, stained, painted, printed, or bleached, and not exceeding thirty threads to the square inch, counting the warp and filling, seven-eighths of one cent per pound and fifteen per centum ad valorem.

344. Bagging for cotton, gunny cloth, and similar fabrics, suitable for covering cotton, composed of single yarns made of jute, jute butts,

or hemp, not bleached, dyed, colored, stained, painted, or printed, not exceeding sixteen threads to the square inch, counting the warp and filling, and weighing not less than fifteen ounces per square yard, six-tenths of one cent per square yard.

345. Handkerchiefs composed of flax, hemp, or ramie, or of which these substances, or either of them, is the component material of chief value, whether in the piece or otherwise, and whether finished or unfinished, not hemmed or hemmed only, fifty per centum ad valorem; if hemstitched, or imitation hemstitched, or revered, or with drawn threads, but not embroidered or initialed, fifty-five per centum ad valorem.

346. Woven fabrics or articles not specially provided for in this Act, composed of flax, hemp, or ramie, or of which these substances or either of them is the component material of chief value, weighing four and one-half ounces or more per square yard, when containing not more than sixty threads to the square inch, counting the warp and filling, one and three-fourths cents per square yard; containing more than sixty and not more than one hundred and twenty threads to the square inch, two and three-fourths cents per square yard; containing more than one hundred and twenty and not more than one hundred and eighty threads to the square inch, six cents per square yard; containing more than one hundred and eighty threads to the square inch, nine cents per square yard, and in addition thereto, on all the foregoing, thirty per centum ad valorem: *Provided*, That none of the foregoing articles in this paragraph shall pay a less rate of duty than fifty per centum ad valorem. Woven fabrics of flax, hemp, or ramie, or of which these substances or either of them is the component material of chief value, including such as is known as shirting cloth, weighing less than four and one-half ounces per square yard and containing more than one hundred threads to the square inch, counting the warp and filling, thirty-five per centum ad valorem.

347. All manufactures of flax, hemp, ramie, or other vegetable fiber, or of which these substances, or either of them, is the component material of chief value, not specially provided for in this Act, forty-five per centum ad valorem.

SCHEDULE K.—WOOL AND MANUFACTURES OF WOOL.

348. All wools, hair of the camel, goat, alpaca, and other like animals shall be divided, for the purpose of fixing the duties to be charged thereon, into the three following classes:

349. Class one, that is to say, merino, mestiza, metz, or metis wools, or other wools of Merino blood, immediate or remote, Down clothing wools, and wools of like character with any of the preceding, including Bagdad wool, China lamb's wool, Castel Branco, Adrianople skin wool or butcher's wool, and such as have been heretofore usually imported into the United States from Buenos Ayres, New Zealand, Australia, Cape of Good Hope, Russia, Great Britain, Canada, Egypt, Morocco, and elsewhere, and all wools not hereinafter included in classes two and three.

350. Class two, that is to say, Leicester, Cotswold, Lincolnshire, Down combing wools, Canada long wools, or other like combing wools of English blood, and usually known by the terms herein used, and also hair of the camel, Angora goat, alpaca, and other like animals.

351. Class three, that is to say, Donskoi, native South American, Cordova, Valparaiso, native Smyrna, Russian camel's hair, and all such

wools of like character as have been heretofore usually imported into the United States from Turkey, Greece, Syria, and elsewhere, excepting improved wools hereinafter provided for.

352. The standard samples of all wools which are now or may be hereafter deposited in the principal custom-houses of the United States, under the authority of the Secretary of the Treasury, shall be the standards for the classification of wools under this Act, and the Secretary of the Treasury is authorized to renew these standards and to make such additions to them from time to time as may be required, and he shall cause to be deposited like standards in other custom-houses of the United States when they may be needed.

353. Whenever wools of class three shall have been improved by the admixture of Merino or English blood, from their present character as represented by the standard samples now or hereafter to be deposited in the principal custom-houses of the United States, such improved wools shall be classified for duty either as class one or as class two, as the case may be.

354. The duty on wools of the first class which shall be imported washed shall be twice the amount of the duty to which they would be subjected if imported unwashed; and the duty on wools of the first and second classes which shall be imported scoured shall be three times the duty to which they would be subjected if imported unwashed. The duty on wools of the third class, if imported in condition for use in carding or spinning into yarns, or which shall not contain more than eight per cent of dirt or other foreign substance, shall be three times the duty to which they would otherwise be subjected.

355. Unwashed wools shall be considered such as shall have been shorn from the sheep without any cleansing; that is, in their natural condition. Washed wools shall be considered such as have been washed with water only on the sheep's back, or on the skin. Wools of the first and second classes washed in any other manner than on the sheep's back or on the skin shall be considered as scoured wool.

356. The duty upon wool of the sheep or hair of the camel, Angora goat, alpaca, and other like animals, of class one and class two, which shall be imported in any other than ordinary condition, or which has been sorted or increased in value by the rejection of any part of the original fleece, shall be twice the duty to which it would be otherwise subject: *Provided*, That skirted wools as imported in eighteen hundred and ninety and prior thereto are hereby excepted. The duty upon wool of the sheep or hair of the camel, Angora goat, alpaca, and other like animals of any class which shall be changed in its character or condition for the purpose of evading the duty, or which shall be reduced in value by the admixture of dirt or any other foreign substance, shall be twice the duty to which it would be otherwise subject. When the duty assessed upon any wool equals three times or more that which would be assessed if said wool was imported unwashed, the duty shall not be doubled on account of the wool being sorted. If any bale or package of wool or hair specified in this Act invoiced or entered as of any specified class, or claimed by the importer to be dutiable as of any specified class, shall contain any wool or hair subject to a higher rate of duty than the class so specified, the whole bale or package shall be subject to the highest rate of duty chargeable on wool of the class subject to such higher rate of duty, and if any bale or package be claimed by the importer to be shoddy, mungo, flocks, wool, hair, or other material of any class specified in this Act, and such bale contain any admixture of any one or more of said materials, or of any other material, the whole

bale or package shall be subject to duty at the highest rate imposed upon any article in said bale or package.

357. The duty upon all wools and hair of the first class shall be eleven cents per pound, and upon all wools or hair of the second class twelve cents per pound.

358. On wools of the third class and on camel's hair of the third class the value whereof shall be twelve cents or less per pound, the duty shall be four cents per pound.

359. On wools of the third class, and on camel's hair of the third class, the value whereof shall exceed twelve cents per pound, the duty shall be seven cents per pound.

360. The duty on wools on the skin shall be one cent less per pound than is imposed in this schedule on other wools of the same class and condition, the quantity and value to be ascertained under such rules as the Secretary of the Treasury may prescribe.

361. Top waste, slubbing waste, roving waste, ring waste, and garnetted waste, thirty cents per pound.

362. Shoddy, twenty-five cents per pound; noils, wool extract, yarn waste, thread waste, and all other wastes composed wholly or in part of wool, and not specially provided for in this Act, twenty cents per pound.

363. Woolen rags, mungo, and flocks, ten cents per pound.

364. Wool and hair which have been advanced in any manner or by any process of manufacture beyond the washed or scoured condition, not specially provided for in this Act, shall be subject to the same duties as are imposed upon manufactures of wool not specially provided for in this Act.

365. On yarns made wholly or in part of wool, valued at not more than thirty cents per pound, the duty per pound shall be two and one-half times the duty imposed by this Act on one pound of unwashed wool of the first class; valued at more than thirty cents per pound, the duty per pound shall be three and one-half times the duty imposed by this Act on one pound of unwashed wool of the first class, and in addition thereto, upon all the foregoing, forty per centum ad valorem.

366. On cloths, knit fabrics, and all manufactures of every description made wholly or in part of wool, not specially provided for in this Act, valued at not more than forty cents per pound, the duty per pound shall be three times the duty imposed by this Act on a pound of unwashed wool of the first class; valued at above forty cents per pound and not above seventy cents per pound, the duty per pound shall be four times the duty imposed by this Act on one pound of unwashed wool of the first class, and in addition thereto, upon all the foregoing, fifty per centum ad valorem; valued at over seventy cents per pound, the duty per pound shall be four times the duty imposed by this Act on one pound of unwashed wool of the first class and fifty-five per centum ad valorem.

367. On blankets, and flannels for underwear composed wholly or in part of wool, valued at not more than forty cents per pound, the duty per pound shall be the same as the duty imposed by this Act on two pounds of unwashed wool of the first class, and in addition thereto thirty per centum ad valorem; valued at more than forty cents and not more than fifty cents per pound, the duty per pound shall be three times the duty imposed by this Act on one pound of unwashed wool of the first class, and in addition thereto thirty-five per centum ad valorem. On blankets composed wholly or in part of wool, valued at more than fifty cents per pound, the duty per pound shall be three times the duty

imposed by this Act on one pound of unwashed wool of the first class, and in addition thereto forty per centum ad valorem. Flannels composed wholly or in part of wool, valued at above fifty cents per pound, shall be classified and pay the same duty as women's and children's dress goods, coat linings, Italian cloths, and goods of similar character and description provided by this Act: *Provided*, That on blankets over three yards in length the same duties shall be paid as on cloths.

368. On women's and children's dress goods, coat linings, Italian cloths, and goods of similar description and character of which the warp consists wholly of cotton or other vegetable material with the remainder of the fabric composed wholly or in part of wool, valued at not exceeding fifteen cents per square yard, the duty shall be seven cents per square yard; valued at more than fifteen cents per square yard, the duty shall be eight cents per square yard; and in addition thereto on all the foregoing valued at not above seventy cents per pound, fifty per centum ad valorem; valued above seventy cents per pound, fifty-five per centum ad valorem: *Provided*, That on all the foregoing, weighing over four ounces per square yard, the duty shall be the same as imposed by this schedule on cloths.

369. On women's and children's dress goods, coat linings, Italian cloths, bunting, and goods of similar description or character composed wholly or in part of wool, and not specially provided for in this Act, the duty shall be eleven cents per square yard; and in addition thereto on all the foregoing valued at not above seventy cents per pound, fifty per centum ad valorem; valued above seventy cents per pound, fifty-five per centum ad valorem: *Provided*, That on all the foregoing, weighing over four ounces per square yard, the duty shall be the same as imposed by this schedule on cloths.

370. On clothing, ready-made, and articles of wearing apparel of every description, including shawls whether knitted or woven, and knitted articles of every description, made up or manufactured wholly or in part, felts not woven and not specially provided for in this Act, composed wholly or in part of wool, the duty per pound shall be four times the duty imposed by this Act on one pound of unwashed wool of the first class, and in addition thereto sixty per centum ad valorem.

371. Webbings, gorings, suspenders, braces, bandings, beltings, bindings, braids, galloons, edgings, insertings, flouncings, fringes, gimps, cords, cords and tassels, laces and other trimmings and articles made wholly or in part of lace, embroideries and articles embroidered by hand or machinery, head nets, netting, buttons or barrel buttons or buttons of other forms for tassels or ornaments, and manufactures of wool ornamented with beads or spangles of whatever material composed, any of the foregoing made of wool or of which wool is a component material, whether composed in part of india-rubber or otherwise, fifty cents per pound and sixty per centum ad valorem.

372. Aubusson, Axminster, moquette, and chenille carpets, figured or plain, and all carpets or carpeting of like character or description, sixty cents per square yard, and in addition thereto forty per centum ad valorem.

373. Saxony, Wilton, and Tournay velvet carpets, figured or plain, and all carpets or carpeting of like character or description, sixty cents per square yard, and in addition thereto forty per centum ad valorem.

374. Brussels carpets, figured or plain, and all carpets or carpeting of like character or description, forty-four cents per square yard, and in addition thereto forty per centum ad valorem.

375. Velvet and tapestry velvet carpets, figured or plain, printed on

the warp or otherwise, and all carpets or carpeting of like character or description, forty cents per square yard, and in addition thereto forty per centum ad valorem.

376. Tapestry Brussels carpets, figured or plain, and all carpets or carpeting of like character or description, printed on the warp or otherwise, twenty-eight cents per square yard, and in addition thereto forty per centum ad valorem.

377. Treble ingrain, three-ply, and all chain Venetian carpets, twenty-two cents per square yard, and in addition thereto forty per centum ad valorem.

378. Wool Dutch and two-ply ingrain carpets, eighteen cents per square yard, and in addition thereto forty per centum ad valorem.

379. Carpets of every description woven whole for rooms, and Oriental, Berlin, Aubusson, Axminster, and similar rugs, ten cents per square foot and in addition thereto, forty per centum ad valorem.

380. Druggets and bockings, printed, colored, or otherwise, twenty-two cents per square yard, and in addition thereto forty per centum ad valorem.

381. Carpets and carpeting of wool, flax, or cotton, or composed in part of either, not specially provided for in this Act, fifty per centum ad valorem.

382. Mats, rugs for floors, screens, covers, hassocks, bed sides, art squares, and other portions of carpets or carpeting made wholly or in part of wool, and not specially provided for in this Act, shall be subjected to the rate of duty herein imposed on carpets or carpetings of like character or description.

383. Whenever, in any schedule of this Act, the word "wool" is used in connection with a manufactured article of which it is a component material, it shall be held to include wool or hair of the sheep, camel, goat, alpaca or other animal, whether manufactured by the woolen, worsted, felt, or any other process.

SCHEDULE L.—SILKS AND SILK GOODS.

384. Silk partially manufactured from cocoons or from waste silk, and not further advanced or manufactured than carded or combed silk, forty cents per pound.

385. Thrown silk, not more advanced than singles, tram, organzine, sewing silk, twist, floss, and silk threads or yarns of every description, except spun silk, thirty per centum ad valorem; spun silk in skeins, cops, warps, or on beams, valued at not exceeding one dollar per pound, twenty cents per pound and fifteen per centum ad valorem; valued at over one dollar per pound and not exceeding one dollar and fifty cents per pound, thirty cents per pound and fifteen per centum ad valorem; valued at over one dollar and fifty cents per pound and not exceeding two dollars per pound, forty cents per pound and fifteen per centum ad valorem; valued at over two dollars per pound and not exceeding two dollars and fifty cents per pound, fifty cents per pound and fifteen per centum ad valorem; valued at over two dollars and fifty cents per pound, sixty cents per pound and fifteen per centum ad valorem; but in no case shall the foregoing articles pay a less rate of duty than thirty-five per centum ad valorem.

386. Velvets, velvet or plush ribbons, chenilles, or other pile fabrics, cut or uncut, composed of silk, or of which silk is the component material of chief value, not specially provided for in this Act, one dollar and fifty cents per pound and fifteen per centum ad valorem;

plushes, composed of silk, or of which silk is the component material of chief value, one dollar per pound and fifteen per centum ad valorem; but in no case shall the foregoing articles pay a less rate of duty than fifty per centum ad valorem.

387. Woven fabrics in the piece, not specially provided for in this Act, weighing not less than one and one-third ounces per square yard and not more than eight ounces per square yard, and containing not more than twenty per centum in weight of silk, if in the gum, fifty cents per pound, and if dyed in the piece, sixty cents per pound; if containing more than twenty per centum and not more than thirty per centum in weight of silk, if in the gum, sixty-five cents per pound, and if dyed in the piece, eighty cents per pound; if containing more than thirty per centum and not more than forty-five per centum in weight of silk, if in the gum, ninety cents per pound, and if dyed in the piece, one dollar and ten cents per pound; if dyed in the thread or yarn and containing not more than thirty per centum in weight of silk, if black (except selvedges), seventy-five cents per pound, and if other than black, ninety cents per pound; if containing more than thirty and not more than forty-five per centum in weight of silk, if black (except selvedges), one dollar and ten cents per pound, and if other than black, one dollar and thirty cents per pound; if containing more than forty-five per centum in weight of silk, or if composed wholly of silk, if dyed in the thread or yarn and weighted in the dyeing so as to exceed the original weight of the raw silk, if black (except selvedges), one dollar and fifty cents per pound, and if other than black, two dollars and twenty-five cents per pound; if dyed in the thread or yarn, and the weight is not increased by dyeing beyond the original weight of the raw silk, three dollars per pound; if in the gum, two dollars and fifty cents per pound; if boiled off, or dyed in the piece, or printed, three dollars per pound; if weighing less than one and one-third ounces and more than one-third of an ounce per square yard, if in the gum, or if dyed in the thread or yarn, two and one-half dollars per pound; if weighing less than one and one-third ounces and more than one-third of an ounce per square yard, if boiled off, three dollars per pound; if dyed or printed in the piece, three dollars and twenty-five cents per pound; if weighing not more than one-third of an ounce per square yard, four dollars and fifty cents per pound; but in no case shall any of the foregoing fabrics in this paragraph pay a less rate of duty than fifty per centum ad valorem.

388. Handkerchiefs or mufflers composed wholly or in part of silk, whether in the piece or otherwise, finished or unfinished, if not hemmed or hemmed only, shall pay the same rate of duty as is imposed on goods in the piece of the same description, weight, and condition as provided for in this schedule; but such handkerchiefs or mufflers shall not pay a less rate of duty than fifty per centum ad valorem; if such handkerchiefs or mufflers are hemstitched or imitation hemstitched, or revered or have drawn threads, or are embroidered in any manner, whether with an initial letter, monogram, or otherwise, by hand or machinery, or are tamboured, appliqued, or are made or trimmed wholly or in part with lace, or with tucking or insertion, they shall pay a duty of ten per centum ad valorem in addition to the duty hereinbefore prescribed, and in no case less than sixty per centum ad valorem.

389. Bandings, including hat bands, beltings, bindings, bone casings, braces, cords, cords and tassels, garters, gorings, suspenders, tubings, and webs and webbings, composed wholly or in part of silk, and whether composed in part of india-rubber or otherwise, if not embroidered in any manner by hand or machinery, fifty per centum ad valorem.

390. Laces, and articles made wholly or in part of lace, edgings, insertings, galloons, chiffon or other flouncings, nets or nettings and veilings, neck rufflings, ruchings, braids, fringes, trimmings, embroideries and articles embroidered by hand or machinery, or tamboured or appliqued, clothing ready made, and articles of wearing apparel of every description, including knit goods, made up or manufactured in whole or in part by the tailor, seamstress, or manufacturer; all of the above-named articles made of silk, or of which silk is the component material of chief value, not specially provided for in this Act, and silk goods ornamented with beads or spangles, of whatever material composed, sixty per centum ad valorem: *Provided,* That any wearing apparel or other articles provided for in this paragraph (except gloves) when composed in part of india-rubber, shall be subject to a duty of sixty per centum ad valorem.

391. All manufactures of silk, or of which silk is the component material of chief value, including such as have india-rubber as a component material, not specially provided for in this Act, and all Jacquard figured goods in the piece, made on looms, of which silk is the component material of chief value, dyed in the yarn, and containing two or more colors in the filling, fifty per centum ad valorem: *Provided,* That all manufactures, of which wool is a component material, shall be classified and assessed for duty as manufactures of wool.

392. In ascertaining the weight of silk under the provisions of this schedule, the weight shall be taken in the condition in which found in the goods, without deduction therefrom for any dye, coloring matter, or other foreign substance or material.

Schedule M.—Pulp, Papers, and Books.

Pulp and Paper:
393. Mechanically ground wood pulp, one-twelfth of one cent per pound, dry weight; chemical wood pulp, unbleached, one-sixth of one cent per pound, dry weight; bleached, one-fourth of one cent per pound, dry weight: *Provided,* That if any country or dependency shall impose an export duty on pulp wood exported to the United States, the amount of such export duty shall be added, as an additional duty, to the duties herein imposed upon wood pulp, when imported from such country or dependency.
394. Sheathing paper and roofing felt, ten per centum ad valorem.
395. Filter masse or filter stock, composed wholly or in part of wood pulp, wood flour, cotton or other vegetable fiber, one and one-half cents per pound and fifteen per centum ad valorem.
396. Printing paper, unsized, sized or glued, suitable for books and newspapers, valued at not above two cents per pound, three-tenths of one cent per pound; valued above two cents and not above two and one-half cents per pound, four-tenths of one cent per pound; valued above two and one-half cents per pound and not above three cents per pound, five-tenths of one cent per pound; valued above three cents and not above four cents per pound, six-tenths of one cent per pound; valued above four cents and not above five cents per pound, eight-tenths of one cent per pound; valued above five cents per pound, fifteen per centum ad valorem: *Provided,* That if any country or dependency shall impose an export duty upon pulp wood exported to the United States, there shall be imposed upon printing paper

when imported from such country or dependency, an additional duty of one-tenth of one cent per pound for each dollar of export duty per cord so imposed, and proportionately for fractions of a dollar of such export duty.

397. Papers commonly known as copying paper, stereotype paper, paper known as bibulous paper, tissue paper, pottery paper, and all similar papers, white, colored or printed, weighing not over six pounds to the ream of four hundred and eighty sheets, on a basis of twenty by thirty inches, and whether in reams or any other form, six cents per pound and fifteen per centum ad valorem; if weighing over six pounds and not over ten pounds to the ream, and letter copying books, whether wholly or partly manufactured, five cents per pound and fifteen per centum ad valorem; crepe paper and filtering paper, five cents per pound and fifteen per centum ad valorem.

398. Surface-coated papers not specially provided for in this Act, two and one-half cents per pound and fifteen per centum ad valorem; if printed, or wholly or partly covered with metal or its solutions, or with gelatin or flock, three cents per pound and twenty per centum ad valorem; parchment papers, two cents per pound and ten per centum ad valorem; plain basic photographic papers for albumenizing, sensitizing, or baryta coating, three cents per pound and ten per centum ad valorem; albumenized or sensitized paper or paper otherwise surface coated for photographic purposes, thirty per centum ad valorem.

MANUFACTURES OF PAPER:

399. Paper envelopes, plain, twenty per centum ad valorem; if bordered, embossed, printed, tinted, or decorated, thirty-five per centum ad valorem.

400. Lithographic prints from stone, zinc, aluminum or other material, bound or unbound (except cigar labels, flaps, and bands, lettered, or otherwise, music and illustrations when forming a part of a periodical or newspaper and accompanying the same, or if bound in or forming a part of printed books, not specially provided for in this Act), on paper or other material not exceeding eight one-thousandths of one inch in thickness, twenty cents per pound ; on paper or other material exceeding eight one-thousandths of one inch and not exceeding twenty one-thousandths of one inch in thickness, and exceeding thirty-five square inches, but not exceeding four hundred square inches cutting size in dimensions, eight cents per pound ; exceeding four hundred square inches cutting size in dimensions, thirty-five per centum ad valorem; prints exceeding eight one-thousandths of one inch and not exceeding twenty one-thousandths of one inch in thickness, and not exceeding thirty-five square inches cutting size in dimensions, five cents per pound; lithographic prints from stone, zinc, aluminum or other material, on cardboard or other material, exceeding twenty one-thousandths of one inch in thickness, six cents per pound; lithographic cigar labels, flaps and bands, lettered or blank, printed from stone, zinc, aluminum or other material, if printed in less than eight colors (bronze printing to be counted as two colors), but not including labels, flaps and bands printed in whole or in part in metal leaf, twenty cents

per pound. Labels, flaps and bands, if printed entirely in bronze printing, fifteen cents per pound; labels, flaps and bands printed in eight or more colors, but not including labels, flaps and bands printed in whole or in part in metal leaf, thirty cents per pound; labels, flaps and bands printed in whole or in part in metal leaf, fifty cents per pound. Books of paper or other material for children's use, containing illuminated lithographic prints, not exceeding in weight twenty-four ounces each, and all booklets and fashion magazines or periodicals printed in whole or in part by lithographic process or decorated by hand, eight cents per pound.

401. Writing, letter, note, hand-made, drawing, ledger, bond, record, tablet, and typewriter paper, weighing not less than ten pounds and not more than fifteen pounds to the ream, two cents per pound and ten per centum ad valorem; weighing more than fifteen pounds to the ream, three and one-half cents per pound and fifteen per centum ad valorem; but if any such paper is ruled, bordered, embossed, printed, or decorated in any manner, it shall pay ten per centum ad valorem in addition to the foregoing rates: *Provided*, That in computing the duty on such paper every one hundred and eighty thousand square inches shall be taken to be a ream.

402. Paper hangings and paper for screens or fireboards, and all other paper not specially provided for in this Act, twenty-five per centum ad valorem; all Jacquard designs of one line paper, or parts of such designs, finished or unfinished, thirty-five per centum ad valorem; all Jacquard designs cut on Jacquard cards, or parts of such designs, finished or unfinished, thirty-five per centum ad valorem.

MANUFACTURES OF PAPER:

403. Books of all kinds, including blank books and pamphlets, and engravings bound or unbound, photographs, etchings, maps, charts, music in books or sheets, and printed matter, all the foregoing not specially provided for in this Act, twenty-five per centum ad valorem.

404. Photograph, autograph, and scrap albums, wholly or partly manufactured, thirty-five per centum ad valorem.

405. All fancy boxes made of paper, or of which paper is the component material of chief value, or if covered with surface-coated paper, forty-five per centum ad valorem.

406. Playing cards, in packs not exceeding fifty-four cards and at a like rate for any number in excess, ten cents per pack and twenty per centum ad valorem.

407. Manufactures of paper, or of which paper is the component material of chief value, not specially provided for in this Act, thirty-five per centum ad valorem.

SCHEDULE N.—SUNDRIES.

408. Beads of all kinds, not threaded or strung, thirty-five per centum ad valorem; fabrics, nets or nettings, laces, embroideries, galloons, wearing apparel, ornaments, trimmings and other articles not specially provided for in this Act, composed wholly or in part of beads or spangles made of glass or paste, gelatin, metal, or other material, but not composed in part of wool, sixty per centum ad valorem.

409. Braids, plaits, laces, and willow sheets or squares, composed wholly of straw, chip, grass, palm leaf, willow, osier, or rattan, suitable for making or ornamenting hats, bonnets, or hoods, not bleached, dyed, colored or stained, fifteen per centum ad valorem; if bleached, dyed, colored or stained, twenty per centum ad valorem; hats, bonnets, and hoods, composed of straw, chip, grass, palm leaf, willow, osier, or rattan, whether wholly or partly manufactured, but not trimmed, thirty-five per centum ad valorem; if trimmed, fifty per centum ad valorem. But the terms "grass" and "straw" shall be understood to mean these substances in their natural form and structure, and not the separated fiber thereof.

410. Brushes, brooms and feather dusters of all kinds, and hair pencils in quills or otherwise, forty per centum ad valorem.

411. Bristles, sorted, bunched or prepared, seven and one-half cents per pound.

BUTTONS AND BUTTON FORMS:

412. Trousers buckles made wholly or partly of iron or steel, or parts thereof, valued at not more than fifteen cents per hundred, five cents per hundred; valued at more than fifteen cents per hundred and not more than fifty cents per hundred, ten cents per hundred; valued at more than fifty cents per hundred, fifteen cents per hundred; and in addition thereto on each and all of the above buckles or parts of buckles, fifteen per centum ad valorem.

413. Button forms: Lastings, mohair, cloth, silk, or other manufactures of cloth, woven or made in patterns of such size, shape, or form, or cut in such manner as to be fit for buttons exclusively, ten per centum ad valorem.

414. Buttons or parts of buttons and button molds or blanks, finished or unfinished, shall pay duty at the following rates, the line button measure being one-fortieth of one inch, namely: Buttons known commercially as agate buttons, metal trousers buttons, (except steel), and nickel bar buttons, one-twelfth of one cent per line per gross; buttons of bone, and steel trousers buttons, one-fourth of one cent per line per gross; buttons of pearl or shell, one and one-half cents per line per gross; buttons of horn, vegetable ivory, glass, or metal, not specially provided for in this Act, three-fourths of one cent per line per gross, and in addition thereto, on all the foregoing articles in this paragraph, fifteen per centum ad valorem; shoe buttons made of paper, board, papier mache, pulp or other similar material, not specially provided for in this Act, valued at not exceeding three cents per gross, one cent per gross; buttons not specially provided for in this Act, and all collar or cuff buttons and studs, fifty per centum ad valorem.

415. Coal, bituminous, and all coals containing less than ninety-two per centum of fixed carbon, and shale, sixty-seven cents per ton of twenty-eight bushels, eighty pounds to the bushel; coal slack or culm, such as will pass through a half-inch screen, fifteen cents per ton of twenty-eight bushels, eighty pounds to the bushel: *Provided*, That on all coal imported into the United States, which is afterwards used for fuel on board vessels propelled by steam and engaged in trade with foreign countries, or in trade between the Atlantic and Pacific ports of the United States, and which are registered under the laws of the United States, a drawback shall be allowed equal to the duty imposed by law upon such coal, and shall be paid under such regulations as the

Secretary of the Treasury shall prescribe; coke, twenty per centum ad valorem.

416. Cork bark, cut into squares or cubes, eight cents per pound: manufactured corks over three-fourths of an inch in diameter measured at larger end, fifteen cents per pound; three-fourths of an inch and less in diameter, measured at larger end, twenty-five cents per pound; cork, artificial, or cork substitutes, manufactured from cork waste and not otherwise provided for, eight cents per pound.

417. Dice, draughts, chessmen, chess balls, and billiard, pool, and bagatelle balls, of ivory, bone, or other materials, fifty per centum ad valorem.

418. Dolls, doll heads, toy marbles of whatever materials composed, and all otner toys not composed of rubber, china, porcelain, parian, bisque, earthen or stone ware, and not specially provided for in this Act, thirty-five per centum ad valorem.

419. Emery grains, and emery manufactured, ground, pulverized, or refined, one cent per pound; emery wheels, emery files, and manufactures of which emery is the component material of chief value, twenty-five per centum ad valorem.

EXPLOSIVE SUBSTANCES:

420. Firecrackers of all kinds, eight cents per pound, the weight to include all coverings, wrappings, and packing material.

421. Fulminates, fulminating powders, and like articles, not specially provided for in this Act, thirty per centum ad valorem.

422. Gunpowder, and all explosive substances used for mining, blasting, artillery, or sporting purposes, when valued at twenty cents or less per pound, four cents per pound; valued above twenty cents per pound, six cents per pound.

423. Matches, friction or lucifer, of all descriptions, per gross of one hundred and forty-four boxes, containing not more than one hundred matches per box, eight cents per gross; when imported otherwise than in boxes containing not more than one hundred matches each, one cent per one thousand matches.

424. Percussion caps, thirty per centum ad valorem; cartridges, thirty-five per centum ad valorem; blasting caps, two dollars and thirty-six cents per one thousand caps.

425. Feathers and downs of all kinds, including bird skins or parts thereof with the feathers on, crude or not dressed, colored, or otherwise advanced or manufactured in any manner, not specially provided for in this Act, fifteen per centum ad valorem; when dressed, colored, or otherwise advanced or manufactured in any manner, including quilts of down and other manufactures of down, and also dressed and finished birds suitable for millinery ornaments, and artificial or ornamental feathers, fruits, grains, leaves, flowers, and stems or parts thereof, of whatever material composed, not specially provided for in this Act, fifty per centum ad valorem.

426. Furs, dressed on the skin but not made up into articles, and furs not on the skin, prepared for hatters' use, including fur skins carroted, twenty per centum ad valorem.

427. Fans of all kinds, except common palm-leaf fans, fifty per centum ad valorem.

428. Gun wads of all descriptions, twenty per centum ad valorem.

429. Hair, human, if clean or drawn but not manufactured, twenty per centum ad valorem.

430. Hair, curled, suitable for beds or mattresses, ten per centum ad valorem.

431. Haircloth, known as "crinoline" cloth, ten cents per square yard; haircloth, known as "hair seating," and hair press cloth, twenty cents per square yard.

432. Hats, bonnets, or hoods, for men's, women's, boys', or children's wear, trimmed or untrimmed, including bodies, hoods, plateaux, forms, or shapes, for hats or bonnets, composed wholly or in chief value of fur of the rabbit, beaver, or other animals, valued at not more than five dollars per dozen, two dollars per dozen; valued at more than five dollars per dozen and not more than ten dollars per dozen, three dollars per dozen; valued at more than ten dollars per dozen and not more than twenty dollars per dozen, five dollars per dozen; valued at more than twenty dollars per dozen, seven dollars per dozen; and in addition thereto on all the foregoing, twenty per centum ad valorem.

433. Indurated fiber ware and manufactures of wood or other pulp, and not otherwise specially provided for, thirty-five per centum ad valorem.

JEWELRY AND PRECIOUS STONES:

434. Articles commonly known as jewelry, and parts thereof, finished or unfinished, not specially provided for in this Act, including precious stones set, pearls set or strung, and cameos in frames, sixty per centum ad valorem.

435. Diamonds and other precious stones advanced in condition or value from their natural state by cleaving, splitting, cutting, or other process, and not set, ten per centum ad valorem; imitations of diamonds or other precious stones, composed of glass or paste, not exceeding an inch in dimensions, not engraved, painted, or otherwise ornamented or decorated, and not mounted or set, twenty per centum ad valorem.

436. Pearls in their natural state, not strung or set, ten per centum ad valorem.

LEATHER, AND MANUFACTURES OF:

437. Hides of cattle, raw or uncured, whether dry, salted, or pickled, fifteen per centum ad valorem: *Provided*, That upon all leather exported, made from imported hides, there shall be allowed a drawback equal to the amount of duty paid on such hides, to be paid under such regulations as the Secretary of the Treasury may prescribe.

438. Band or belting leather, sole leather, dressed upper and all other leather, calfskins tanned or tanned and dressed, kangaroo, sheep and goat skins (including lamb and kid skins) dressed and finished, chamois and other skins and bookbinders' calfskins, all the foregoing not specially provided for in this Act, twenty per centum ad valorem; skins for morocco, tanned but unfinished, ten per centum ad valorem; patent, japanned, varnished or enameled leather, weighing not over ten pounds per dozen hides or skins, thirty cents per pound and twenty per centum ad valorem; if weighing over ten pounds and not over twenty-five pounds per dozen, thirty cents per pound and ten per centum ad valorem; if weighing over twenty-five pounds per dozen, twenty cents per pound and ten per centum ad valorem; pianoforte leather and pianoforte action leather, thirty-five per centum ad valorem; leather shoe laces, finished or unfinished, fifty cents per gross pairs and twenty per centum ad valorem; boots and shoes made of leather,

twenty-five per centum ad valorem: *Provided*, That leather cut into shoe uppers or vamps or other forms, suitable for conversion into manufactured articles, shall be classified as manufactures of leather and pay duty accordingly.

Gloves—

439. Gloves made wholly or in part of leather, whether wholly or partly manufactured, shall pay duty at the following rates, the lengths stated in each case being the extreme length when stretched to their full extent, namely:

440. Women's or children's "glace" finish, Schmaschen (of sheep origin), not over fourteen inches in length, one dollar and seventy-five cents per dozen pairs; over fourteen inches and not over seventeen inches in length, two dollars and twenty-five cents per dozen pairs; over seventeen inches in length, two dollars and seventy-five cents per dozen pairs; men's "glace" finish, Schmaschen (sheep), three dollars per dozen pairs.

441. Women's or children's "glace" finish, lamb or sheep, not over fourteen inches in length, two dollars and fifty cents per dozen pairs; over fourteen and not over seventeen inches in length, three dollars and fifty cents per dozen pairs; over seventeen inches in length, four dollars and fifty cents per dozen pairs; men's "glace" finish, lamb or sheep, four dollars per dozen pairs.

442. Women's or children's "glace" finish, goat, kid, or other leather than of sheep origin, not over fourteen inches in length, three dollars per dozen pairs; over fourteen and not over seventeen inches in length, three dollars and seventy-five cents per dozen pairs; over seventeen inches in length, four dollars and seventy-five cents per dozen pairs; men's "glace" finish, kid, goat, or other leather than of sheep origin, four dollars per dozen pairs.

443. Women's or children's, of sheep origin, with exterior grain surface removed, by whatever name known, not over seventeen inches in length, two dollars and fifty cents per dozen pairs; over seventeen inches in length, three dollars and fifty cents per dozen pairs; men's, of sheep origin, with exterior surface removed, by whatever name known, four dollars per dozen pairs.

444. Women's or children's kid, goat, or other leather than of sheep origin, with exterior grain surface removed, by whatever name known, not over fourteen inches in length, three dollars per dozen pairs; over fourteen inches and not over seventeen inches in length, three dollars and seventy-five cents per dozen pairs; over seventeen inches in length, four dollars and seventy-five cents per dozen pairs; men's, goat, kid, or other leather than of sheep origin, with exterior grain surface removed, by whatever name known, four dollars per dozen pairs.

445. In addition to the foregoing rates there shall be paid the following cumulative duties: On all leather gloves, when lined, one dollar per dozen pairs; on all pique or prix seam gloves, forty cents per dozen pairs; on all gloves stitched or embroidered, with more than three single strands or cords, forty cents per dozen pairs.

446. Glove tranks, with or without the usual accompanying pieces, shall pay seventy-five per centum of the duty provided for the gloves in the fabrication of which they are suitable.

447. Harness, saddles and saddlery, or parts of either, in sets or in parts, finished or unfinished, forty-five per centum ad valorem.

MISCELLANEOUS MANUFACTURES:

448. Manufactures of amber, asbestos, bladders, cork, catgut or whip gut or worm gut, or wax, or of which these substances or either of them is the component material of chief value, not specially provided for in this Act, twenty-five per centum ad valorem.

449. Manufactures of bone, chip, grass, horn, india-rubber, palm leaf, straw, weeds, or whalebone, or of which these substances or either of them is the component material of chief value, not specially provided for in this Act, thirty per centum ad valorem; but the terms "grass" and "straw" shall be understood to mean these substances in their natural form and structure, and not the separated fiber thereof.

450. Manufactures of leather, finished or unfinished, manufactures of fur, gelatin, gutta-percha, human hair, ivory, vegetable ivory, mother-of-pearl and shell, plaster of paris, papier mâché, and vulcanized india-rubber known as "hard rubber," or of which these substances or either of them is the component material of chief value, not specially provided for in this Act, and shells engraved, cut, ornamented, or otherwise manufactured, thirty-five per centum ad valorem.

451. Masks, composed of paper or pulp, thirty-five per centum ad valorem.

452. Matting made of cocoa fiber or rattan, six cents per square yard; mats made of cocoa fiber or rattan, four cents per square foot.

453. Musical instruments or parts thereof, pianoforte actions and parts thereof, strings for musical instruments not otherwise enumerated, cases for musical instruments, pitch pipes, tuning forks, tuning hammers, and metronomes; strings for musical instruments, composed wholly or in part of steel or other metal, all the foregoing, forty-five per centum ad valorem.

454. Paintings in oil or water colors, pastels, pen and ink drawings, and statuary, not specially provided for in this Act, twenty per centum ad valorem; but the term "statuary" as used in this Act shall be understood to include only such statuary as is cut, carved, or otherwise wrought by hand from a solid block or mass of marble, stone, or alabaster, or from metal, and as is the professional production of a statuary or sculptor only.

455. Peat moss, one dollar per ton.

456. Pencils of paper or wood filled with lead or other material, and pencils of lead, forty-five cents per gross and twenty-five per centum ad valorem; slate pencils, covered with wood, thirty-five per centum ad valorem; all other slate pencils, three cents per one hundred.

457. Pencil leads not in wood, ten per centum ad valorem.

458. Photographic dry plates or films, twenty-five per centum ad valorem.

459. Pipes and smokers' articles: Common tobacco pipes and pipe bowls made wholly of clay, valued at not more than forty cents per gross, fifteen cents per gross; other tobacco pipes and pipe bowls of clay, fifty cents per gross and twenty-five per centum ad valorem; other pipes and pipe bowls of whatever material composed, and all smokers' articles whatsoever, not specially provided for in this Act, including cigarette books, cigarette book covers, pouches for smoking or chewing tobacco, and cigarette paper in all forms, sixty per centum ad valorem.

460. Plows, tooth and disk harrows, harvesters, reapers, agricultural drills, and planters, mowers, horserakes, cultivators, threshing machines and cotton gins, twenty per centum ad valorem.

461. Plush, black, known commercially as hatters' plush, composed of silk, or of silk and cotton, such as is used exclusively for making men's hats, ten per centum ad valorem.

462. Umbrellas, parasols, and sun shades covered with material other than paper, fifty per centum ad valorem. Sticks for umbrellas, parasols, or sun shades, and walking canes, finished or unfinished, forty per centum ad valorem.

463. Waste, not specially provided for in this Act, ten per centum ad valorem.

FREE LIST.

SEC. 2. That on and after the passage of this Act, unless otherwise specially provided for in this Act, the following articles when imported shall be exempt from duty:

464. Acids: Arsenic or arsenious, benzoic, carbolic, fluoric, hydrochloric or muriatic, nitric, oxalic, phosphoric, phthalic, picric or nitropicric, prussic, silicic, and valerianic.

465. Aconite.

466. Acorns, raw, dried or undried, but unground.

467. Agates, unmanufactured.

468. Albumen, not specially provided for.

469. Alizarin, natural or artificial, and dyes derived from alizarin or from anthracin.

470. Amber, and amberoid unmanufactured, or crude gum.

471. Ambergris.

472. Aniline salts.

473. Any animal imported specially for breeding purposes shall be admitted free: *Provided*, That no such animal shall be admitted free unless pure bred of a recognized breed, and duly registered in the book of record established for that breed: *And provided further*, That certificate of such record and of the pedigree of such animal shall be produced and submitted to the customs officer, duly authenticated by the proper custodian of such book of record, together with the affidavit of the owner, agent, or importer that such animal is the identical animal described in said certificate of record and pedigree: *And provided further*, That the Secretary of Agriculture shall determine and certify to the Secretary of the Treasury what are recognized breeds and pure bred animals under the provisions of this paragraph. The Secretary of the Treasury may prescribe such additional regulations as may be required for the strict enforcement of this provision. Cattle, horses, sheep, or other domestic animals straying across the boundary line into any foreign country, or driven across such boundary line by the owner for temporary pasturage purposes only, together with their offspring, may be brought back to the United States within six months free of duty, under regulations to be prescribed by the Secretary of the Treasury.

474. Animals brought into the United States temporarily for a period not exceeding six months, for the purpose of exhibition or competition for prizes offered by any agricultural or racing association; but a bond shall be given in accordance with regulations prescribed by the Secretary of the Treasury; also teams of animals, including their harness and tackle and the wagons or other vehicles actually owned by persons

emigrating from foreign countries to the United States with their families, and in actual use for the purpose of such emigration under such regulations as the Secretary of the Treasury may prescribe; and wild animals intended for exhibition in zoological collections for scientific and educational purposes, and not for sale or profit.

475. Annatto, roucou, rocoa, or orleans, and all extracts of.

476. Antimony ore, crude sulphite of.

477. Apatite.

478. Arrowroot in its natural state and not manufactured.

479. Arsenic and sulphide of, or orpiment.

480. Arseniate of aniline.

481. Art educational stops, composed of glass and metal and valued at not more than six cents per gross.

482. Articles in a crude state used in dyeing or tanning not specially provided.for in this Act.

483. Articles the growth, produce, and manufacture of the United States, when returned after having been exported, without having been advanced in value or improved in condition by any process of manufacture or other means; casks, barrels, carboys, bags, and other vessels of American manufacture exported filled with American products, or exported empty and returned filled with foreign products, including shooks and staves when returned as barrels or boxes; also quicksilver flasks or bottles, of either domestic or foreign manufacture, which shall have been actually exported from the United States; but proof of the identity of such articles shall be made, under general regulations to be prescribed by the Secretary of the Treasury, but the exemption of bags from duty shall apply only to such domestic bags as may be imported by the exporter thereof, and if any such articles are subject to internal tax at the time of exportation, such tax shall be proved to have been paid before exportation and not refunded: *Provided*, That this paragraph shall not apply to any article upon which an allowance of drawback has been made, the reimportation of which is hereby prohibited except upon payment of duties equal to the drawbacks allowed; or to any article manufactured in bonded warehouse and exported under any provision of law: *And provided further*, That when manufactured tobacco which has been exported without payment of internal-revenue tax shall be reimported it shall be retained in the custody of the collector of customs until internal-revenue stamps in payment of the legal duties shall be placed thereon.

484. Asbestos, unmanufactured.

485. Ashes, wood and lye of, and beet-root ashes.

486. Asafetida.

487. Balm of Gilead.

488. Barks, cinchona or other from which quinine may be extracted.

489. Baryta, carbonate of, or witherite.

490. Beeswax.

491. Binding twine: All binding twine manufactured from New Zealand hemp, istle or Tampico fiber, sisal grass, or sunn, or a mixture of any two or more of them, of single ply and measuring not exceeding six hundred feet to the pound: *Provided*, That articles mentioned in this paragraph if imported from a country which lays an import duty on like articles imported from the United States, shall be subject to a duty of one-half of one cent per pound.

492. Bells, broken, and bell metal broken and fit only to be remanufactured.

493. Birds, stuffed, not suitable for millinery ornaments.

494. Birds and land and water fowls.
495. Bismuth.
496. Bladders, and all integuments and intestines of animals and fish sounds, crude, dried or salted for preservation only, and unmanufactured, not specially provided for in this Act.
497. Blood, dried, not specially provided for.
498. Bolting cloths composed of silk, imported expressly for milling purposes, and so permanently marked as not to be available for any other use.
499. Bones, crude, or not burned, calcined, ground, steamed, or otherwise manufactured, and bone dust or animal carbon, and bone ash, fit only for fertilizing purposes.
500. Books, engravings, photographs, etchings, bound or unbound, maps and charts imported by authority or for the use of the United States or for the use of the Library of Congress.
501. Books, maps, music, engravings, photographs, etchings, bound or unbound, and charts, which shall have been printed more than twenty years at the date of importation, and all hydrographic charts, and publications issued for their subscribers or exchanges by scientific and literary associations or academies, or publications of individuals for gratuitous private circulation, and public documents issued by foreign Governments.
502. Books and pamphlets printed exclusively in languages other than English; also books and music, in raised print, used exclusively by the blind.
503. Books, maps, music, photographs, etchings, lithographic prints, and charts, specially imported, not more than two copies in any one invoice, in good faith, for the use or by order of any society or institution incorporated or established solely for religious, philosophical, educational, scientific, or literary purposes, or for the encouragement of the fine arts, or for the use or by order of any college, academy, school, or seminary of learning in the United States, or any State or public library, and not for sale, subject to such regulations as the Secretary of the Treasury shall prescribe.
504. Books, libraries, usual and reasonable furniture, and similar household effects of persons or families from foreign countries, all the foregoing if actually used abroad by them not less than one year, and not intended for any other person or persons, nor for sale.
505. Brass, old brass, clippings from brass or Dutch metal, all the foregoing, fit only for remanufacture.
506. Brazil paste.
507. Brazilian pebble, unwrought or unmanufactured.
508. Breccia, in block or slabs.
509. Bristles, crude, not sorted, bunched, or prepared.
510. Broom corn.
511. Bullion, gold or silver.
512. Burgundy pitch.
513. Cadmium.
514. Calamine.
515. Camphor, crude.
516. Castor or castoreum.
517. Cat gut, whip gut, or worm gut, unmanufactured.
518. Cerium.
519. Chalk, crude, not ground, precipitated, or otherwise manufactured.
520. Chromate of iron or chromic ore.

521. Civet, crude.

522. Clay: Common blue clay in casks suitable for the manufacture of crucibles.

523. Coal, anthracite, not specially provided for in this Act, and coal stores of American vessels, but none shall be unloaded.

524. Coal tar, crude, pitch of coal tar, and products of coal tar known as dead or creosote oil, benzol, toluol, naphthalin, xylol, phenol, cresol, toluidine, xylidin, cumidin, binitrotoluol, binitrobenzol, benzidin, tolidin, dianisidin, naphtol, naphtylamin, diphenylamin, benzaldehyde, benzyl chloride, resorcin, nitro-benzol, and nitro-toluol; all the foregoing not medicinal and not colors or dyes.

525. Cobalt and cobalt ore.

526. Cocculus indicus.

527. Cochineal.

528. Cocoa, or cacao, crude, and fiber, leaves, and shells of.

529. Coffee.

530. Coins, gold, silver, and copper.

531. Coir, and coir yarn.

532. Copper in plates, bars, ingots, or pigs, and other forms, not manufactured or specially provided for in this Act.

533. Old copper, fit only for manufacture, clipping from new copper, and all composition metal of which copper is a component material of chief value not specially provided for in this Act.

534. Copper, regulus of, and black or coarse copper, and copper cement.

535. Coral, marine, uncut, and unmanufactured.

536. Cork wood, or cork bark, unmanufactured.

537. Cotton, and cotton waste or flocks.

538. Cryolite, or kryolith.

539. Cudbear.

540. Curling stones, or quoits, and curling-stone handles.

541. Curry, and curry powder.

542. Cutch.

543. Cuttlefish bone.

544. Dandelion roots, raw, dried, or undried, but unground.

545. Diamonds and other precious stones, rough or uncut, and not advanced in condition or value from their natural state by cleaving, splitting, cutting, or other process, including miners', glaziers' and engravers' diamonds not set, and diamond dust or bort.

546. Divi-divi.

547. Dragon's blood.

548. Drugs, such as barks, beans, berries, balsams, buds, bulbs, and bulbous roots, excrescences, fruits, flowers, dried fibers, and dried insects, grains, gums, and gum resin, herbs, leaves, lichens, mosses, nuts, nutgalls, roots, and stems, spices, vegetables, seeds aromatic, and seeds of morbid growth, weeds, and woods used expressly for dyeing; any of the foregoing which are drugs and not edible and are in a crude state, and not advanced in value or condition by refining or grinding, or by other process, and not specially provided for in this Act.

549. Eggs of birds, fish, and insects: *Provided, however,* That this shall not be held to include the eggs of game birds or eggs of birds not used for food, the importation of which is prohibited except specimens for scientific collections, nor fish roe preserved for food purposes.

550. Emery ore.

551. Ergot.

552. Fans, common palm-leaf, plain and not ornamented or decorated

in any manner, and palm leaf in its natural state, not colored, dyed, or otherwise advanced or manufactured.

553. Felt, adhesive, for sheathing vessels.

554. Fibrin, in all forms.

555. Fish, fresh, frozen, or packed in ice, caught in the Great Lakes or other fresh waters by citizens of the United States.

556. Fish skins.

557. Flint, flints, and flint stones, unground.

558. Fossils.

559. Fruits or berries, green, ripe, or dried, and fruits in brine, not specially provided for in this Act.

560. Fruit-plants, tropical and semitropical, for the purpose of propagation or cultivation.

561. Furs, undressed.

562. Fur skins of all kinds not dressed in any manner and not specially provided for in this Act.

563. Gambier.

564. Glass enamel, white, for watch and clock dials.

565. Glass plates or discs, rough-cut or unwrought, for use in the manufacture of optical instruments, spectacles, and eye glasses, and suitable only for such use: *Provided, however*, That such discs exceeding eight inches in diameter may be polished sufficiently to enable the character of the glass to be determined.

566. Grasses and fibers: Istle or Tampico fiber, jute, jute butts, manila, sisal grass, sunn, and all other textile grasses or fibrous vegetable substances, not dressed or manufactured in any manner, and not specially provided for in this Act.

567. Gold-beaters' molds and gold-beaters' skins.

568. Grease, and oils (excepting fish oils), such as are commonly used in soap making or in wire drawing, or for stuffing or dressing leather, and which are fit only for such uses, and not specially provided for in this Act.

569. Guano, manures, and all substances used only for manure.

570. Gutta percha, crude.

571. Hair of horse, cattle, and other animals, cleaned or uncleaned, drawn or undrawn, but unmanufactured, not specially provided for in this Act; and human hair, raw, uncleaned, and not drawn.

572. Hide cuttings, raw, with or without hair, and all other glue stock.

573. Hide rope.

574. Hones and whetstones.

575. Hoofs, unmanufactured.

576. Hop roots for cultivation.

577. Horns and parts of, unmanufactured, including horn strips and tips.

578. Ice.

579. India rubber, crude, and milk of, and old scrap or refuse India rubber which has been worn out by use and is fit only for remanufacture.

580. Indigo.

581. Iodine, crude.

582. Ipecac.

583. Iridium.

584. Ivory tusks in their natural state or cut vertically across the grain only, with the bark left intact, and vegetable ivory in its natural state.

585. Jalap.

586. Jet, unmanufactured.

587. Joss stick, or Joss light.
588. Junk, old.
589. Kelp.
590. Kieserite.
591. Kyanite, or cyanite, and kainite.
592. Lac dye, crude, seed, button, stick, and shell.
593. Lac spirits.
594. Lactarene.
595. Lava, unmanufactured.
596. Leeches.
597. Lemon juice, lime juice, and sour orange juice.
598. Licorice root, unground.
599. Lifeboats and life-saving apparatus specially imported by societies incorporated or established to encourage the saving of human life.
600. Lime, citrate of.
601. Lithographic stones, not engraved.
602. Litmus, prepared or not prepared.
603. Loadstones.
604. Madder and munjeet, or Indian madder, ground or prepared, and all extracts of.
605. Magnesite, crude or calcined, not purified.
606. Magnesium, not made up into articles.
607. Manganese, oxide and ore of.
608. Manna.
609. Manuscripts.
610. Marrow, crude.
611. Marshmallow or althea root, leaves or flowers, natural or unmanufactured.
612. Medals of gold, silver, or copper, and other metallic articles actually bestowed as trophies or prizes, and received and accepted as honorary distinctions.
613. Meerschaum, crude or unmanufactured.
614. Minerals, crude, or not advanced in value or condition by refining or grinding, or by other process of manufacture, not specially provided for in this Act.
615. Mineral salts obtained by evaporation from mineral waters, when accompanied by a duly authenticated certificate and satisfactory proof, showing that they are in no way artificially prepared, and are only the product of a designated mineral spring.
616. Models of inventions and of other improvements in the arts, including patterns for machinery, but no article shall be deemed a model or pattern which can be fitted for use otherwise.
617. Moss, seaweeds, and vegetable substances, crude or unmanufactured, not otherwise specially provided for in this Act.
618. Musk, crude, in natural pods.
619. Myrobolans.
620. Needles, hand sewing, and darning.
621. Newspapers and periodicals; but the term "periodicals" as herein used shall be understood to embrace only unbound or paper-covered publications, issued within six months of the time of entry, containing current literature of the day and issued regularly at stated periods, as weekly, monthly, or quarterly.
622. Nuts: Brazil nuts, cream nuts, palm nuts and palm-nut kernels; cocoanuts in the shell and broken cocoanut meat or copra, not shredded, desiccated, or prepared in any manner.
623. Nux vomica.

624. Oakum.

625. Oil cake.

626. Oils: Almond, amber, crude and rectified ambergris, anise or anise seed, aniline, aspic or spike lavender, bergamot, cajeput, caraway, cassia, cinnamon, cedrat, chamomile, citronella or lemon grass, civet, cocoanut, fennel, ichthyol, jasmine or jasimine, juglandium, juniper, lavender, lemon, limes, mace, neroli or orange flower, enfleurage grease, nut oil or oil of nuts not otherwise specially provided for in this Act, orange oil, olive oil for manufacturing or mechanical purposes fit only for such use and valued at not more than sixty cents per gallon, ottar of roses, palm, rosemary or anthoss, sesame or sesamum seed or bean, thyme, origanum red or white, valerian; and also spermaceti, whale, and other fish oils of American fisheries, and all fish and other products, of such fisheries; petroleum, crude or refined: *Provided*, That if there be imported into the United States crude petroleum, or the products of crude petroleum produced in any country which imposes a duty on petroleum or its products exported from the United States, there shall in such cases be levied, paid, and collected a duty upon said crude petroleum or its products so imported equal to the duty imposed by such country.

627. Orange and lemon peel, not preserved, candied, or dried.

628. Orchil, or orchil liquid.

629. Ores of gold, silver, copper, or nickel, and nickel matte; sweepings of gold and silver.

630. Osmium.

631. Palladium.

632. Paper stock, crude, of every description, including all grasses, fibers, rags (other than wool), waste, including jute waste, shavings, clippings, old paper, rope ends, waste rope, and waste bagging, including old gunny cloth and old gunny bags, fit only to be converted into paper.

633. Paraffin.

634. Parchment and vellum.

635. Pearl, mother of, and shells, not sawed, cut, polished or otherwise manufactured, or advanced in value from the natural state.

636. Personal effects, not merchandise, of citizens of the United States dying in foreign countries.

637. Pewter and britannia metal, old, and fit only to be remanufactured.

638. Philosophical and scientific apparatus, utensils, instruments, and preparations, including bottles and boxes containing the same, specially imported in good faith for the use and by order of any society or institution incorporated or established solely for religious, philosophical, educational, scientific, or literary purposes, or for the encouragement of the fine arts, or for the use or by order of any college, academy, school, or seminary of learning in the United States, or any State or public library, and not for sale, subject to such regulations as the Secretary of the Treasury shall prescribe.

639. Phosphates, crude.

640. Plants, trees, shrubs, roots, seed-cane, and seeds, imported by the Department of Agriculture or the United States Botanic Garden.

641. Platina, in ingots, bars, sheets, and wire.

642. Platinum, unmanufactured, and vases, retorts, and other apparatus, vessels, and parts thereof composed of platinum, for chemical uses.

643. Plumbago.

644. Potash, crude, or "black salts"; carbonate of potash, crude or refined; hydrate of, or caustic potash, not including refined in sticks or rolls; nitrate of potash or saltpeter, crude; sulphate of potash, crude or refined, and muriate of potash.

645. Professional books, implements, instruments, and tools of trade, occupation, or employment, in the actual possession at the time, of persons emigrating to the United States; but this exemption shall not be construed to include machinery or other articles imported for use in any manufacturing establishment, or for any other person or persons, or for sale, nor shall it be construed to include theatrical scenery, properties, and apparel; but such articles brought by proprietors or managers of theatrical exhibitions arriving from abroad, for temporary use by them in such exhibitions, and not for any other person, and not for sale, and which have been used by them abroad, shall be admitted free of duty under such regulations as the Secretary of the Treasury may prescribe; but bonds shall be given for the payment to the United States of such duties as may be imposed by law upon any and all such articles as shall not be exported within six months after such importation: *Provided*, That the Secretary of the Treasury may in his discretion extend such period for a further term of six months in case application shall be made therefor.

646. Pulu.

647. Quinia, sulphate of, and all alkaloids or salts of cinchona bark.

648. Rags, not otherwise specially provided for in this Act.

649. Regalia and gems, statuary, and specimens or casts of sculpture, where specially imported in good faith for the use and by order of any society incorporated or established solely for religious, philosophical, educational, scientific, or literary purposes, or for the encouragement of the fine arts, or for the use and by order of any college, academy, school, or seminary of learning in the United States, or any State or public library, and not for sale; but the term "regalia" as herein used shall be held to embrace only such insignia of rank or office or emblems as may be worn upon the person or borne in the hand during public exercises of the society or institution, and shall not include articles of furniture or fixtures, or of regular wearing apparel, nor personal property of individuals.

650. Rennets, raw or prepared.

651. Saffron and safflower, and extract of, and saffron cake.

652. Sago, crude.

653. Salacin.

654. Salep, or salop.

655. Sausages, bologna.

656. Seeds: Anise, caraway, cardamom, cauliflower, coriander, cotton, cummin, fennel, fenugreek, hemp, hoarhound, mangel-wurzel, mustard, rape, Saint John's bread or bean, sugar beet, sorghum or sugar cane for seed; bulbs and bulbous roots, not edible and not otherwise provided for; all flower and grass seeds; all the foregoing not specially provided for in this Act.

657. Sheep dip, not including compounds or preparations that can be used for other purposes.

658. Shotgun barrels, in single tubes, forged, rough bored.

659. Shrimps and other shell fish.

660. Silk, raw, or as reeled from the cocoon, but not doubled, twisted, or advanced in manufacture in any way.

661. Silk cocoons and silk waste.

662. Silkworm's eggs.

663. Skeletons and other preparations of anatomy.

664. Skins of all kinds, raw (except sheepskins with the wool on), and hides not specially provided for in this Act.

665. Soda, nitrate of, or cubic nitrate.

666. Specimens of natural history, botany, and mineralogy, when imported for scientific public collections, and not for sale.

667. Spices: Cassia, cassia vera, and cassia buds; cinnamon and chips of; cloves and clove stems; mace; nutmegs; pepper, black or white, and pimento; all the foregoing when unground; ginger root, unground and not preserved or candied.

668. Spunk.

669. Spurs and stilts used in the manufacture of earthen, porcelain, and stone ware.

670. Stamps; foreign postage or revenue stamps, canceled or uncanceled.

671. Stone and sand: Burrstone in blocks, rough or unmanufactured; cliff stone, unmanufactured; rotten stone, tripoli, and sand, crude or manufactured, not otherwise provided for in this Act.

672. Storax, or styrax.

673. Strontia, oxide of, and protoxide of strontian, and strontianite, or mineral carbonate of strontia.

674. Sulphur, lac or precipitated, and sulphur or brimstone, crude, in bulk, sulphur ore as pyrites, or sulphuret of iron in its natural state, containing in excess of twenty-five per centum of sulphur, and sulphur not otherwise provided for.

675. Sulphuric acid which at the temperature of sixty degrees Fahrenheit does not exceed the specific gravity of one and three hundred and eighty thousandths, for use in manufacturing superphosphate of lime or artificial manures of any kind, or for any agricultural purposes: *Provided*, That upon all sulphuric acid imported from any country, whether independent or a dependency, which imposes a duty upon sulphuric acid imported into such country from the United States, there shall be levied and collected a duty of one-fourth of one cent per pound.

676. Tamarinds.

677. Tapioca, cassava or cassady.

678. Tar and pitch of wood.

679. Tea and tea plants.

680. Teeth, natural, or unmanufactured.

681. Terra alba, not made from gypsum or plaster rock.

682. Terra japonica.

683. Tin ore, cassiterite or black oxide of tin, and tin in bars, blocks, pigs, or grain or granulated.

684. Tobacco stems.

685. Tonquin, tonqua, or tonka beans.

686. Turmeric.

687. Turpentine, Venice.

688. Turpentine, spirits of.

689. Turtles.

690. Types, old, and fit only to be remanufactured.

691. Uranium, oxide and salts of.

692. Vaccine virus.

693. Valonia.

694. Verdigris, or subacetate of copper.

695. Wax, vegetable or mineral.

696. Wafers, unleavened or not edible.

697. Wearing apparel, articles of personal adornment, toilet articles, and similar personal effects of persons arriving in the United States; but this exemption shall only include such articles as actually accompany and are in the use of, and as are necessary and appropriate for the wear and use of such persons, for the immediate purposes of the journey and present comfort and convenience, and shall not be held to apply to merchandise or articles intended for other persons or for sale: *Provided*, That in case of residents of the United States returning from abroad, all wearing apparel and other personal effects taken by them out of the United States to foreign countries shall be admitted free of duty, without regard to their value, upon their identity being established, under appropriate rules and regulations to be prescribed by the Secretary of the Treasury, but no more than one hundred dollars in value of articles purchased abroad by such residents of the United States shall be admitted free of duty upon their return.

698. Whalebone, unmanufactured.

699. Wood: Logs and round unmanufactured timber, including pulp-woods, firewood, handle-bolts, shingle-bolts, gun-blocks for gun-stocks rough-hewn or sawed or planed on one side, hop-poles, ship-timber and ship-planking; all the foregoing not specially provided for in this Act.

700. Woods: Cedar, lignum-vitæ, lancewood, ebony, box, granadilla, mahogany, rosewood, satinwood, and all forms of cabinet woods, in the log, rough, or hewn only; briar root or briar wood and similar wood unmanufactured, or not further advanced than cut into blocks suitable for the articles into which they are intended to be converted; bamboo, rattan, reeds unmanufactured, India malacca joints, and sticks of partridge, hair wood, pimento, orange, myrtle, and other woods not specially provided for in this Act, in the rough, or not further advanced than cut into lengths suitable for sticks for umbrellas, parasols, sunshades, whips, fishing rods, or walking-canes.

701. Works of art, drawings, engravings, photographic pictures, and philosophical and scientific apparatus brought by professional artists, lecturers, or scientists arriving from abroad for use by them temporarily for exhibition and in illustration, promotion, and encouragement of art, science, or industry in the United States, and not for sale, shall be admitted free of duty, under such regulations as the Secretary of the Treasury shall prescribe; but bonds shall be given for the payment to the United States of such duties as may be imposed by law upon any and all such articles as shall not be exported within six months after such importation: *Provided*, That the Secretary of the Treasury may, in his discretion, extend such period for a further term of six months in cases where applications therefor shall be made.

702. Works of art, collections in illustration of the progress of the arts, sciences, or manufactures, photographs, works in terra cotta, parian, pottery, or porcelain, antiquities and artistic copies thereof in metal or other material, imported in good faith for exhibition at a fixed place by any State or by any society or institution established for the encouragement of the arts, science, or education, or for a municipal corporation, and all like articles imported in good faith by any society or association, or for a municipal corporation for the purpose of erecting a public monument, and not intended for sale, nor for any other purpose than herein expressed; but bonds shall be given under such rules and regulations as the Secretary of the Treasury may prescribe, for the payment of lawful duties which may accrue should any of the articles aforesaid be sold, transferred, or used contrary to this provision, and such articles shall be subject, at any time, to examination and inspection by

the proper officers of the customs: *Provided,* That the privileges of this and the preceding section shall not be allowed to associations or corporations engaged in or connected with business of a private or commercial character.

703. Works of art, the production of American artists residing temporarily abroad, or other works of art, including pictorial paintings on glass, imported expressly for presentation to a national institution, or to any State or municipal corporation, or incorporated religious society, college, or other public institution, except stained or painted window-glass or stained or painted glass windows; but such exemption shall be subject to such regulations as the Secretary of the Treasury may prescribe.

704. Yams.

705. Zaffer.

SEC. 3. That for the purpose of equalizing the trade of the United States with foreign countries, and their colonies, producing and exporting to this country the following articles: Argols, or crude tartar, or wine lees, crude; brandies, or other spirits manufactured or distilled from grain or other materials; champagne and all other sparkling wines; still wines, and vermuth; paintings and statuary; or any of them, the President be, and he is hereby, authorized, as soon as may be after the passage of this Act, and from time to time thereafter, to enter into negotiations with the governments of those countries exporting to the United States the above-mentioned articles, or any of them, with a view to the arrangement of commercial agreements in which reciprocal and equivalent concessions may be secured in favor of the products and manufactures of the United States; and whenever the government of any country, or colony, producing and exporting to the United States the above-mentioned articles, or any of them, shall enter into a commercial agreement with the United States, or make concessions in favor of the products, or manufactures thereof, which, in the judgment of the President, shall be reciprocal and equivalent, he shall be, and he is hereby, authorized and empowered to suspend, during the time of such agreement or concession, by proclamation to that effect, the imposition and collection of the duties mentioned in this Act, on such article or articles so exported to the United States from such country or colony, and thereupon and thereafter the duties levied, collected, and paid upon such article or articles shall be as follows, namely:

Argols, or crude tartar, or wine lees, crude, five per centum ad valorem.

Brandies, or other spirits manufactured or distilled from grain or other materials, one dollar and seventy-five cents per proof gallon.

Champagne and all other sparkling wines, in bottles containing not more than one quart and more than one pint, six dollars per dozen; containing not more than one pint each and more than one-half pint, three dollars per dozen; containing one-half pint each or less, one dollar and fifty cents per dozen; in bottles or other vessels containing more than one quart each, in addition to six dollars per dozen bottles on the quantities in excess of one quart, at the rate of one dollar and ninety cents per gallon.

Still wines, and vermuth, in casks, thirty-five cents per gallon; in bottles or jugs, per case of one dozen bottles or jugs containing each not more than one quart and more than one pint, or twenty-four bottles or jugs containing each not more than one pint, one dollar and twenty-five cents per case, and any excess beyond these quantities found in such bottles or jugs shall be subject to a duty of four cents per pint or fractional part thereof, but no separate or additional duty shall be assessed upon the bottles or jugs.

Paintings in oil or water colors, pastels, pen and ink drawings, and statuary, fifteen per centum ad valorem.

The President shall have power, and it shall be his duty, whenever he shall be satisfied that any such agreement in this Section mentioned is not being fully executed by the Government with which it shall have been made, to revoke such suspension and notify such Government thereof.

And it is further provided that with a view to secure reciprocal trade with countries producing the following articles, whenever and so often as the President shall be satisfied that the Government of any country, or colony of such Government, producing and exporting directly or indirectly to the United States coffee, tea, and tonquin, tonqua, or tonka beans, and vanilla beans, or any of such articles, imposes duties or other exactions upon the agricultural, manufactured, or other products of the United States, which, in view of the introduction of such coffee, tea, and tonquin, tonqua, or tonka beans, and vanilla beans, into the United States, as in this Act hereinbefore provided for, he may deem to be reciprocally unequal and unreasonable, he shall have the power and it shall be his duty to suspend, by proclamation to that effect, the provisions of this Act relating to the free introduction of such coffee, tea, and tonquin, tonqua, or tonka beans, and vanilla beans, of the products of such country or colony, for such time as he shall deem just; and in such case and during such suspension duties shall be levied, collected, and paid upon coffee, tea, and tonquin, tonqua, or tonka beans, and vanilla beans, the products or exports, direct or indirect, from such designated country, as follows:

On coffee, three cents per pound.

On tea, ten cents per pound.

On tonquin, tonqua, or tonka beans, fifty cents per pound; vanilla beans, two dollars per pound; vanilla beans, commercially known as cuts, one dollar per pound.

SEC. 4. That whenever the President of the United States, by and with the advice and consent of the Senate, with a view to secure reciprocal trade with foreign countries, shall, within the period of two years from and after the passage of this Act, enter into commercial treaty or treaties with any other country or countries concerning the admission into any such country or countries of the goods, wares, and merchandise of the United States and their use and disposition therein, deemed to be for the interests of the United States, and in such treaty or treaties, in consideration of the advantages accruing to the United States therefrom, shall provide for the reduction during a specified period, not exceeding five years, of the duties imposed by this Act, to the extent of not more than twenty per centum thereof, upon such goods, wares, or merchandise as may be designated therein of the country or countries with which such treaty or treaties shall be made as in this section provided for; or shall provide for the transfer during such period from the dutiable list of this Act to the free list thereof of such goods, wares, and merchandise, being the natural products of such foreign country or countries and not of the United States; or shall provide for the retention upon the free list of this Act during a specified period, not exceeding five years, of such goods, wares, and merchandise now included in said free list as may be designated therein; and when any such treaty shall have been duly ratified by the Senate and approved by Congress, and public proclamation made accordingly, then and thereafter the duties which shall be collected by the United States upon any of the designated goods, wares, and merchandise from the foreign country with which such treaty has been made shall, during the period provided for, be the duties specified and provided for in such treaty, and none other.

SEC. 5. That whenever any country, dependency, or colony shall pay or bestow, directly or indirectly, any bounty or grant upon the exportation of any article or merchandise from such country, dependency, or colony, and such article or merchandise is dutiable under the provisions of this Act, then upon the importation of any such article or merchandise into the United States, whether the same shall be imported directly from the country of production or otherwise, and whether such article or merchandise is imported in the same condition as when exported from the country of production or has been changed in condition by remanufacture or otherwise, there shall be levied and paid, in all such cases, in addition to the duties otherwise imposed by this Act, an additional duty equal to the net amount of such bounty or grant, however the same be paid or bestowed. The net amount of all such bounties or grants shall be from time to time ascertained, determined, and declared by the Secretary of the Treasury, who shall make all needful regulations for the identification of such articles and merchandise and for the assessment and collection of such additional duties.

SEC. 6. That there shall be levied, collected, and paid on the importation of all raw or unmanufactured articles, not enumerated or provided for in this Act, a duty of ten per centum ad valorem, and on all articles manufactured, in whole or in part, not provided for in this Act, a duty of twenty per centum ad valorem.

SEC. 7. That each and every imported article, not enumerated in this Act, which is similar, either in material, quality, texture, or the use to which it may be applied, to any article enumerated in this Act as chargeable with duty, shall pay the same rate of duty which is levied on the enumerated article which it most resembles in any of the particulars before mentioned; and if any nonenumerated article equally resembles two or more enumerated articles on which different rates of duty are chargeable, there shall be levied on such nonenumerated article the same rate of duty as is chargeable on the article which it resembles paying the highest rate of duty; and on articles not enumerated, manufactured of two or more materials, the duty shall be assessed at the highest rate at which the same would be chargeable if composed wholly of the component material thereof of chief value; and the words "component material of chief value," wherever used in this Act, shall be held to mean that component material which shall exceed in value any other single component material of the article; and the value of each component material shall be determined by the ascertained value of such material in its condition as found in the article. If two or more rates of duty shall be applicable to any imported article, it shall pay duty at the highest of such rates.

SEC. 8. That all articles of foreign manufacture, such as are usually or ordinarily marked, stamped, branded, or labeled, and all packages containing such or other imported articles, shall, respectively, be plainly marked, stamped, branded, or labeled in legible English words in a conspicuous place, so as to indicate the country of their origin and the quantity of their contents; and until so marked, stamped, branded, or labeled they shall not be delivered to the importer. Should any article of imported merchandise be marked, stamped, branded, or labeled so as to indicate a quantity, number, or measurement in excess of the quantity, number, or measurement actually contained in such article, no delivery of the same shall be made to the importer until the mark, stamp, brand, or label, as the case may be, shall be changed so as to conform to the facts of the case.

SEC. 9. That section thirty-three hundred and forty-one of the Revised Statutes of the United States be, and hereby is, amended to read as follows:

"SEC. 3341. The Commissioner of Internal Revenue shall cause to be prepared, for the payment of such tax, suitable stamps denoting the amount of tax required to be paid on the hogsheads, barrels, and halves, thirds, quarters, sixths, and eighths of a barrel of such fermented liquors (and shall also cause to be prepared suitable permits for the purpose hereinafter mentioned), and shall furnish the same to the collectors of internal revenue, who shall each be required to keep on hand at all times a sufficient supply of permits and a supply of stamps equal in amount to two months' sales thereof, if there be any brewery or brewery warehouse in his district; and such stamps shall be sold, and permits granted and delivered by such collectors, only to the brewers of their district, respectively.

"Such collectors shall keep an account of the number of permits delivered and of the number and value of the stamps sold by them to each brewer."

SEC. 10. That section thirty-three hundred and ninety-four of the Revised Statutes of the United States, as amended, be, and the same is hereby, further amended, so as to read as follows:

"Upon cigars which shall be manufactured and sold, or removed for consumption or sale, there shall be assessed and collected the following taxes, to be paid by the manufacturer thereof: On cigars of all descriptions made of tobacco, or any substitute therefor, and weighing more than three pounds per thousand, three dollars per thousand; on cigars, made of tobacco, or any substitute therefor, and weighing not more than three pounds per thousand, one dollar per thousand; on cigarettes, made of tobacco, or any substitute therefor, and weighing more than three pounds per thousand, three dollars per thousand; on cigarettes, made of tobacco, or any substitute therefor, and weighing not more than three pounds per thousand, one dollar per thousand: *Provided*, That all rolls of tobacco, or any substitute therefor, wrapped with tobacco, shall be classed as cigars, and all rolls of tobacco, or any substitute therefor, wrapped in paper or any substance other than tobacco, shall be classed as cigarettes.

"And the Commissioner of Internal Revenue, with the approval of the Secretary of the Treasury, shall provide dies and adhesive stamps for cigars weighing not more than three pounds per thousand: *Provided*, That such stamps shall be in denominations of ten, twenty, fifty, and one hundred, and the laws and regulations governing the packing and removal for sale of cigarettes, and the affixing and canceling of the stamps on the packages thereof, shall apply to cigars weighing not more than three pounds per thousand.

"None of the packages of smoking tobacco and fine-cut chewing tobacco and cigarettes prescribed by law shall be permitted to have packed in, or attached to, or connected with, them, any article or thing whatsoever, other than the manufacturers' wrappers and labels, the internal revenue stamp and the tobacco or cigarettes, respectively, put up therein, on which tax is required to be paid under the internal revenue laws; nor shall there be affixed to, or branded, stamped, marked, written, or printed upon, said packages, or their contents, any promise or offer of, or any order or certificate for, any gift, prize, premium, payment, or reward."

Sec. 11. That no article of imported merchandise which shall copy or simulate the name or trade-mark of any domestic manufacture or manufacturer, or which shall bear a name or mark, which is calculated to induce the public to believe that the article is manufactured in the United States, shall be admitted to entry at any custom-house of the United States. And in order to aid the officers of the customs in enforcing this prohibition, any domestic manufacturer who has adopted trademarks may require his name and residence and a description of his trade-marks to be recorded in books which shall be kept for that purpose in the Department of the Treasury, under such regulations as the Secretary of the Treasury shall prescribe, and may furnish to the Department facsimiles of such trade-marks; and thereupon the Secretary of the Treasury shall cause one or more copies of the same to be transmitted to each collector or other proper officer of the customs.

Sec. 12. That all materials of foreign production which may be necessary for the construction of vessels built in the United States for foreign account and ownership, or for the purpose of being employed in the foreign trade, including the trade between the Atlantic and Pacific ports of the United States, and all such materials necessary for the building of their machinery, and all articles necessary for their outfit and equipment, may be imported in bond under such regulations as the Secretary of the Treasury may prescribe; and upon proof that such materials have been used for such purposes no duties shall be paid thereon. But vessels receiving the benefit of this section shall not be allowed to engage in the coastwise trade of the United States more than two months in any one year except upon the payment to the United States of the duties of which a rebate is herein allowed: *Provided*, That vessels built in the United States for foreign account and ownership shall not be allowed to engage in the coastwise trade of the United States.

Sec. 13. That all articles of foreign production needed for the repair of American vessels engaged in foreign trade, including the trade between the Atlantic and Pacific ports of the United States, may be withdrawn from bonded warehouses free of duty, under such regulations as the Secretary of the Treasury may prescribe.

Sec. 14. That the sixteenth section of an Act entitled "An Act to remove certain burdens on the American merchant marine and encourage the American foreign carrying trade, and for other purposes," approved June twenty-sixth, eighteen hundred and eighty four, be amended so as to read as follows:

"Sec. 16. That all articles of foreign or domestic production needed and actually withdrawn from bonded warehouses and bonded manufacturing warehouses for supplies (not including equipment) of vessels of the United States engaged in foreign trade, or in trade between the Atlantic and Pacific ports of the United States, may be so withdrawn from said bonded warehouses, free of duty or of internal-revenue tax, as the case may be, under such regulations as the Secretary of the Treasury may prescribe; but no such articles shall be landed at any port of the United States."

Sec. 15. That all articles manufactured in whole or in part of imported materials, or of materials subject to internal-revenue tax, and intended for exportation without being charged with duty, and without having an internal-revenue stamp affixed thereto, shall, under such regulations as the Secretary of the Treasury may prescribe, in order to be so manufactured and exported, be made and manufactured in bonded warehouses similar to those known and designated in Treasury Regulations as bonded warehouses, class six: *Provided*, That the manufacturer of such articles shall first give satisfactory bonds for the faithful observance of all the provisions of law and of such regulations as shall be prescribed by the Secretary of the Treasury: *Provided further*, That the manufacture of distilled spirits from grain, starch, molasses or sugar, including all dilutions or mixtures of them or either of them, shall not be permitted in such manufacturing warehouses.

Whenever goods manufactured in any bonded warehouse established under the provisions of the preceding paragraph shall be exported directly therefrom or shall be duly laden for transportation and immediate exportation under the supervision of the proper officer who shall be duly designated for that purpose, such goods shall be exempt from duty and from the requirements relating to revenue stamps.

Any materials used in the manufacture of such goods, and any packages, coverings, vessels, brands, and labels used in putting up the same may, under the regulations of the Secretary of the Treasury, be conveyed without the payment of revenue tax or duty into any bonded manufacturing warehouse, and imported goods may, under the aforesaid regulations, be transferred without the exaction of duty from any bonded warehouse into any bonded manufacturing warehouse; but this privilege shall not be held to apply to implements, machinery, or apparatus to be used in the construction or repair of any bonded manufacturing warehouse or for the prosecution of the business carried on therein.

No articles or materials received into such bonded manufacturing warehouse shall be withdrawn or removed therefrom except for direct shipment and exportation or for transportation and immediate exportation in bond under the supervision of the officer duly designated therefor by the collector of the port, who shall certify to such shipment and exportation, or ladening for transportation, as the case may be, describing the articles by their mark or otherwise, the quantity, the date of exportation, and the name of the vessel. All labor performed and services rendered under these provisions shall be under the supervision of a duly designated officer of the customs and at the expense of the manufacturer.

A careful account shall be kept by the collector of all merchandise delivered by him to any bonded manufacturing warehouse, and a sworn monthly return, verified by the customs officers in charge, shall be made by the manufacturers containing a detailed statement of all imported merchandise used by him in the manufacture of exported articles.

Before commencing business the proprietor of any manufacturing warehouse shall file with the Secretary of the Treasury a list of all the articles intended to be manufactured in such warehouse, and state the formula of manufacture and the names and quantities of the ingredients to be used therein.

Articles manufactured under these provisions may be withdrawn under such regulations as the Secretary of the Treasury may prescribe for transportation and delivery into any bonded warehouse at an exterior port for the sole purpose of immediate export therefrom.

The provisions of Revised Statutes thirty-four hundred and thirty-three shall, so far as may be practicable, apply to any bonded manufacturing warehouse established under this Act and to the merchandise conveyed therein.

SEC. 16. That all persons are prohibited from importing into the

United States from any foreign country any obscene book, pamphlet, paper, writing, advertisement, circular, print, picture, drawing, or other representation, figure, or image on or of paper or other material, or any cast, instrument, or other article of an immoral nature, or any drug or medicine, or any article whatever for the prevention of conception or for causing unlawful abortion, or any lottery ticket or any advertisement of any lottery. No such articles, whether imported separately or contained in packages with other goods entitled to entry, shall be admitted to entry; and all such articles shall be proceeded against, seized, and forfeited by due course of law. All such prohibited articles and the package in which they are contained in the course of importation shall be detained by the officer of customs, and proceedings taken against the same as hereinafter prescribed, unless it appears to the satisfaction of the collector of customs that the obscene articles contained in the package were inclosed therein without the knowledge or consent of the importer, owner, agent, or consignee: *Provided,* That the drugs hereinbefore mentioned, when imported in bulk and not put up for any of the purposes hereinbefore specified, are excepted from the operation of this section.

SEC. 17. That whoever, being an officer, agent, or employee of the Government of the United States, shall knowingly aid or abet any person engaged in any violation of any of the provisions of law prohibiting importing, advertising, dealing in, exhibiting, or sending or receiving by mail obscene or indecent publications or representations, or means for preventing conception or procuring abortion, or other articles of indecent or immoral use or tendency, shall be deemed guilty of a misdemeanor, and shall for every offense be punishable by a fine of not more than five thousand dollars, or by imprisonment at hard labor for not more than ten years, or both.

SEC. 18. That any judge of any district or circuit court of the United States, within the proper district, before whom complaint in writing of any violation of the two preceding sections is made, to the satisfaction of such judge, and founded on knowledge or belief, and if upon belief, setting forth the grounds of such belief, and supported by oath or affirmation of the complainant, may issue, conformably to the Constitution, a warrant directed to the marshal or any deputy marshal in the proper district, directing him to search for, seize, and take possession of any such article or thing mentioned in the two preceding sections, and to make due and immediate return thereof to the end that the same may be condemned and destroyed by proceedings, which shall be conducted in the same manner as other proceedings in the case of municipal seizure, and with the same right of appeal or writ of error.

SEC. 19. That machinery for repair may be imported into the United States without payment of duty, under bond, to be given in double the appraised value thereof, to be withdrawn and exported after said machinery shall have been repaired; and the Secretary of the Treasury is authorized and directed to prescribe such rules and regulations as may be necessary to protect the revenue against fraud and secure the identity and character of all such importations when again withdrawn and exported, restricting and limiting the export and withdrawal to the same port of entry where imported, and also limiting all bonds to a period of time of not more than six months from the date of the importation.

SEC. 20. That the produce of the forests of the State of Maine upon the Saint John River and its tributaries, owned by American citizens, and sawed or hewed in the Province of New Brunswick by American citizens, the same being otherwise unmanufactured in whole or in part, which is now admitted into the ports of the United States free of duty, shall continue to be so admitted, under such regulations as the Secretary of the Treasury shall from time to time prescribe.

SEC. 21. That the produce of the forests of the State of Maine upon the Saint Croix River and its tributaries owned by American citizens, and sawed or hewed in the Province of New Brunswick by American citizens, the same being otherwise unmanufactured in whole or in part, shall be admitted into the ports of the United States free of duty, under such regulations as the Secretary of the Treasury shall from time to time prescribe.

SEC. 22. That a discriminating duty of ten per centum ad valorem, in addition to the duties imposed by law, shall be levied, collected, and paid on all goods, wares, or merchandise which shall be imported in vessels not of the United States, or which being the production or manufacture of any foreign country not contiguous to the United States, shall come into the United States from such contiguous country; but this discriminating duty shall not apply to goods, wares, or merchandise which shall be imported in vessels not of the United States, entitled at the time of such importation by treaty or convention to be entered in the ports of the United States on payment of the same duties as shall then be payable on goods, wares, and merchandise imported in vessels of the United States, nor to such foreign products or manufactures as shall be imported from such contiguous countries in the usual course of strictly retail trade.

SEC. 23. That no goods, wares, or merchandise, unless in cases provided for by treaty, shall be imported into the United States from any foreign port or place, except in vessels of the United States, or in such foreign vessels as truly and wholly belong to the citizens or subjects of that country of which the goods are the growth, production, or manufacture, or from which such goods, wares, or merchandise can only be, or most usually are, first shipped for transportation. All goods, wares, or merchandise imported contrary to this section, and the vessel wherein the same shall be imported, together with her cargo, tackle, apparel, and furniture, shall be forfeited to the United States; and such goods, wares, or merchandise, ship, or vessel, and cargo shall be liable to be seized, prosecuted, and condemned in like manner, and under the same regulations, restrictions, and provisions as have been heretofore established for the recovery, collection, distribution, and remission of forfeitures to the United States by the several revenue laws.

SEC. 24. That the preceding section shall not apply to vessels or goods, wares, or merchandise imported in vessels of a foreign nation which does not maintain a similar regulation against vessels of the United States.

SEC. 25. That the importation of neat cattle and the hides of neat cattle from any foreign country into the United States is prohibited: *Provided*, That the operation of this section shall be suspended as to any foreign country or countries, or any parts of such country or countries, whenever the Secretary of the Treasury shall officially determine, and give public notice thereof that such importation will not tend to the introduction or spread of contagious or infectious diseases among the cattle of the United States; and the Secretary of the Treasury is hereby authorized and empowered, and it shall be his duty, to make all necessary orders and regulations to carry this section into effect, or to suspend the same as herein provided, and to send copies thereof to the proper officers in the United States, and to such officers or agents of the United States in foreign countries as he shall judge necessary.

SEC. 26. That any person convicted of a willful violation of any of the provisions of the preceding section shall be fined not exceeding five hundred dollars, or imprisoned not exceeding one year, or both, in the discretion of the court.

SEC. 27. That upon the reimportation of articles once exported, of the growth, product, or manufacture of the United States, upon which no internal tax has been assessed or paid, or upon which such tax has been paid and refunded by allowance or drawback, there shall be levied, collected, and paid a duty equal to the tax imposed by the internal-revenue laws upon such articles, except articles manufactured in bonded warehouses and exported pursuant to law, which shall be subject to the same rate of duty as if originally imported.

SEC. 28. That whenever any vessel laden with merchandise, in whole or in part subject to duty, has been sunk in any river, harbor, bay, or waters subject to the jurisdiction of the United States, and within its limits, for the period of two years, and is abandoned by the owner thereof, any person who may raise such vessel shall be permitted to bring any merchandise recovered therefrom into the port nearest to the place where such vessel was so raised free from the payment of any duty thereupon, but under such regulations as the Secretary of the Treasury may prescribe.

SEC. 29. That the works of manufacturers engaged in smelting or refining metals, or both smelting and refining, in the United States may be designated as bonded warehouses under such regulations as the Secretary of the Treasury may prescribe: *Provided*, That such manufacturers shall first give satisfactory bonds to the Secretary of the Treasury. Ores or metals in any crude form requiring smelting or refining to make them readily available in the arts, imported into the United States to be smelted or refined and intended to be exported in a refined but unmanufactured state, shall, under such rules as the Secretary of the Treasury may prescribe, and under the direction of the proper officer, be removed in original packages or in bulk from the vessel or other vehicle on which they have been imported, or from the bonded warehouse in which the same may be, into the bonded warehouse in which such smelting or refining, or both, may be carried on, for the purpose of being smelted or refined, or both, without payment of duties thereon, and may there be smelted or refined, together with other metals of home or foreign production: *Provided*, That each day a quantity of refined metal equal to ninety per centum of the amount of imported metal smelted or refined that day shall be set aside, and such metal so set aside shall not be taken from said works except for transportation to another bonded warehouse or for exportation, under the direction of the proper officer having charge thereof as aforesaid, whose certificate, describing the articles by their marks or otherwise, the quantity, the date of importation, and the name of vessel or other vehicle by which it was imported, with such additional particulars as may from time to time be required, shall be received by the collector of customs as sufficient evidence of the exportation of the metal, or it may be removed under such regulations as the Secretary of the Treasury may prescribe, upon entry and payment of duties, for domestic consumption, and the exportation of the ninety per centum of metals hereinbefore provided for shall entitle the ores and metals imported under the provisions of this section to admission without payment of the duties thereon: *Provided further*, That in respect to lead ores imported under the provisions of this section the refined metal set aside shall either be reexported or the regular duties paid thereon within six months from the date of the receipt of the ore. All labor performed and services rendered under these regulations shall be under the supervision of an officer of the customs, to be appointed by the Secretary of the Treasury, and at the expense of the manufacturer.

SEC. 30. That where imported materials on which duties have been paid are used in the manufacture of articles manufactured or produced in the United States, there shall be allowed on the exportation of such articles a drawback equal in amount to the duties paid on the materials used, less one per centum of such duties: *Provided,* That when the articles exported are made in part from domestic materials the imported materials, or the parts of the articles made from such materials, shall so appear in the completed articles that the quantity or measure thereof may be ascertained: *And provided further,* That the drawback on any article allowed under existing law shall be continued at the rate herein provided. That the imported materials used in the manufacture or production of articles entitled to drawback of customs duties when exported shall, in all cases where drawback of duties paid on such materials is claimed, be identified, the quantity of such materials used and the amount of duties paid thereon shall be ascertained, the facts of the manufacture or production of such articles in the United States and their exportation therefrom shall be determined, and the drawback due thereon shall be paid to the manufacturer, producer, or exporter, to the agent of either or to the person to whom such manufacturer, producer, exporter, or agent shall in writing order such drawback paid, under such regulations as the Secretary of the Treasury shall prescribe.

SEC. 31. That all goods, wares, articles, and merchandise manufactured wholly or in part in any foreign country by convict labor shall not be entitled to entry at any of the ports of the United States, and the importation thereof is hereby prohibited, and the Secretary of the Treasury is authorized and directed to prescribe such regulations as may be necessary for the enforcement of this provision.

SEC. 32. That sections seven and eleven of the Act entitled "An Act to simplify the laws in relation to the collection of the revenues," approved June tenth, eighteen hundred and ninety, be, and the same are hereby, amended so as to read as follows:

SEC. 7. That the owner, consignee, or agent of any imported merchandise which has been actually purchased may, at the time when he shall make and verify his written entry of such merchandise, but not afterwards, make such addition in the entry to the cost or value given in the invoice or pro forma invoice or statement in form of an invoice, which he shall produce with his entry, as in his opinion may raise the same to the actual market value or wholesale price of such merchandise at the time of exportation to the United States, in the principal markets of the country from which the same has been imported; but no such addition shall be made upon entry to the invoice value of any imported merchandise obtained otherwise than by actual purchase; and the collector within whose district any merchandise may be imported or entered, whether the same has been actually purchased or procured otherwise than by purchase, shall cause the actual market value or wholesale price of such merchandise to be appraised; and if the appraised value of any article of imported merchandise subject to an ad valorem duty or to a duty based upon or regulated in any manner by the value thereof shall exceed the value declared in the entry, there shall be levied, collected, and paid, in addition to the duties imposed by law on such merchandise, an additional duty of one per centum of the total appraised value thereof for each one per centum that such appraised value exceeds the value declared in the entry, but the additional duties shall only apply to the particular article or articles in each invoice that are so undervalued, and shall be limited to fifty per centum of the appraised value of such article or articles. Such additional duties shall not be construed to be penal, and shall not be remitted, nor payment thereof in any way avoided, except in cases arising from a manifest clerical error, nor shall they be refunded in case of exportation of the merchandise, or on any other account, nor shall they be subject to the benefit of drawback: *Provided*, That if the appraised value of any merchandise shall exceed the value declared in the entry by more than fifty per centum, except when arising from a manifest clerical error, such entry shall be held to be presumptively fraudulent, and the collector of customs shall seize such merchandise and proceed as in case of forfeiture for violation of the customs laws, and in any legal proceeding that may result from such seizure, the undervaluation as shown by the appraisal shall be presumptive evidence of fraud, and the burden of proof shall be on the claimant to rebut the same and forfeiture shall be adjudged unless he shall rebut such presumption of fraudulent intent by sufficient evidence. The forfeiture provided for in this section shall apply to the whole of the merchandise or the value thereof in the case or package containing the particular article or articles in each invoice which are undervalued: *Provided, further*, That all additional duties, penalties or forfeitures applicable to merchandise entered by a duly certified invoice, shall be alike applicable to merchandise entered by a pro forma invoice or statement in the form of an invoice, and no forfeiture or disability of any kind, incurred under the provisions of this section shall be remitted or mitigated by the Secretary of the Treasury. The duty shall not, however, be assessed in any case upon an amount less than the invoice or entered value.

SEC. 11. That, when the actual market value as defined by law, of any article of imported merchandise, wholly or partly manufactured and subject to an ad valorem duty, or to a duty based in whole or in part on value, can not be otherwise ascertained to the satisfaction of the appraising officer, such officer shall use all available means in his power to ascertain the cost of production of such merchandise at the time of exportation to the United States, and at the place of manufacture; such cost of production to include the cost of materials and of fabrication, all general expenses covering each and every outlay of whatsoever nature incident to such production, together with the expense of preparing and putting up such merchandise ready for shipment, and an addition of not less than eight nor more than fifty per centum upon the total cost as thus ascertained; and in no case shall such merchandise be appraised upon original appraisal or reappraisement at less than the total cost of production as thus ascertained. It shall be lawful for appraising officers, in determining the dutiable value of such merchandise, to take into consideration the wholesale price at which such or similar merchandise is sold or offered for sale in the United States, due allowance being made for estimated duties thereon, the cost of transportation, insurance, and other necessary expenses from the place of shipment to the United States, and a reasonable commission, if any has been paid, not exceeding six per centum.

SEC. 33. That on and after the day when this Act shall go into effect all goods, wares, and merchandise previously imported, for which no entry has been made, and all goods, wares, and merchandise previously entered without payment of duty and under bond for warehousing, transportation, or any other purpose, for which no permit of delivery to the importer or his agent has been issued, shall be subjected to the duties imposed by this Act and to no other duty, upon the entry or the withdrawal thereof: *Provided*, That when duties are based upon the weight of merchandise deposited in any public or private bonded warehouse, said duties shall be levied and collected upon the weight of such merchandise at the time of its entry.

SEC. 34. That sections one to twenty-four, both inclusive, of an Act entitled "An Act to reduce taxation, to provide revenue for the Government, and for other purposes," which became a law on the twenty-eighth day of August, eighteen hundred and ninety-four, and all acts and parts of acts inconsistent with the provisions of this Act are hereby repealed, said repeal to take effect on and after the passage of this Act, but the repeal of existing laws or modifications thereof embraced in this Act shall not affect any act done, or any right accruing or accrued, or any suit or proceeding had or commenced in any civil cause before the said repeal or modifications; but all rights and liabilities under said laws shall continue and may be enforced in the same manner as if said repeal or modifications had not been made. Any offenses committed and all penalties or forfeitures or liabilities incurred prior to the passage of this Act under any statute embraced in or changed, modified, or repealed by this Act may be prosecuted or punished in the same manner and with the same effect as if this Act had not been passed. All Acts of limitation, whether applicable to civil causes and proceedings or to the prosecution of offenses or for the recovery of penalties or forfeitures embraced in or modified, changed, or repealed by this Act shall not be affected thereby; and all suits, proceedings, or prosecutions, whether civil or criminal, for causes arising or acts done or committed prior to the passage of this Act may be commenced and prosecuted within the same time and with the same effect as if this Act had not been passed: *And provided further*, That nothing in this Act shall be construed to repeal the provisions of section three thousand and fifty-eight of the Revised Statutes as amended by the Act approved February twenty-third, eighteen hundred and eighty-seven, in respect to the abandonment of merchandise to underwriters or the salvors of property, and the ascertainment of duties thereon: *And provided further*, That nothing in this Act shall be construed to repeal or in any manner affect the sections numbered seventy-three, seventy-four, seventy-five, seventy-six, and seventy-seven of an Act entitled "An Act to reduce taxation, to provide revenue for the Government, and for other purposes," which became a law on the twenty-eighth day of August, eighteen hundred and ninety-four.

Approved, July 24, 1897.

www.ingramcontent.com/pod-product-compliance
Lightning Source LLC
Chambersburg PA
CBHW021530270326
41930CB00008B/1182